The Zen Monk and the Blossoming Lotus Flower

*55 Stories for Stress Relief,
Conquering Negativity, Discovering Joy,
and Embracing Your Ideal Life*

Hosa Smith-Zen

ISBN - 9798863246703

Contents

Introduction

In the serene lap of Japan's ancient temples and atop its cloud-swept mountains, generations of Zen monks have devoted themselves to understanding the very essence of existence. With every breath taken in meditation, every leaf observed in its fall, and every raindrop heard on the temple's roof, these monks have gleaned profound insights, seeking a wisdom that goes beyond words and touches the soul.

"The Zen Monk and the Blossoming Wisdom" draws upon this rich tapestry of enlightenment, presenting 55 tales that act as windows into this profound realm of understanding. These stories, deeply rooted in age-old traditions, are not just tales from a bygone era; they are pulsating heartbeats, resonating with timeless life lessons that cater to the modern soul's yearnings. Each narrative, whether it's of Zenji's contemplations or the melodies of the natural world, is a beacon guiding us toward introspection. They beckon us to ponder on life's intricacies, urging us to find a haven of peace amidst the tumult of our modern lives. The protagonists are not heroes in the traditional sense but reflectors, illuminating our own strengths, vulnerabilities, dreams, and doubts.

But as you delve into these tales, I encourage you not to rush. The essence of Zen is in the experience, not just comprehension. Read, but more importantly, feel. Let every story be a meditation. Absorb its essence, let it simmer in your thoughts, and give it the space to touch your heart. Ponder its lesson, imagine its setting, and let its characters converse with your innermost self. This journey is as much about self-discovery as it is about understanding the world around us. Each story is a stepping stone, and the spaces in between are where you'll find reflections, not just of the tales, but of your own life. How does each lesson resonate with your experiences?

How can it guide your decisions, shape your perceptions, or inspire your aspirations?

In today's world, where moments fly by and screens dominate our attention, taking the time to pause, reflect, and truly immerse in these tales might be the most radical act you can undertake. It is in this stillness that you'll find the blossoming wisdom these stories promise. May this collection of stories be more than just a book to you. Let it be a companion on your journey toward stress relief, an ally in conquering negativity, a guide to discovering joy, and a mentor in embracing your ideal life. The journey may be long, but with every page turned, you're one step closer.

May the whispers of Zen wisdom guide you, inspire you, and light your path.

1

Zenji, the Willow, and Resilience's Whisper

enji, a humble monk in his early fifties, lived by the banks of a crystalline river that snaked through a tranquil village. On one side of the river stood the village with its bustling markets, cheerful children, and the ever-present hum of activity. On the opposite side was a haven of natural serenity a meadow dotted with wildflowers, leading to a grove where a majestic willow stood, its branches gracefully draped over the sparkling waters. Every morning, after his meditations, Zenji would walk to the willow, finding solace in its presence. The village elders often spoke of the tree, recounting tales passed down through generations. They said the willow had been there longer than the village itself, witnessing countless seasons change, watching over the village like a gentle guardian.

One summer, a severe drought struck the region. Crops failed, wells dried up, and the once clear river trickled slowly, reducing in its breadth and vigor. The villagers grew anxious, fearing that the prolonged drought might force them to leave their ancestral homes. Zenji, too, was concerned but for a different reason. Each day, he watched the willow, noticing its leaves turn a shade yellower, its bark slightly more brittle. Yet, the willow did not wither away. Instead, it seemed to stand even taller, its roots presumably delving deeper into the earth, seeking the water it so desperately needed.

On a particularly scorching day, Zenji noticed a group of village children at the grove. They were attempting to break off branches from the willow, believing that its wood, when burned, would bring rain according to an old village myth. Zenji approached them calmly, "My dear children, do you hear the whispers of the tree?" The children stopped, looking at each other and then at Zenji with puzzled eyes. "It's just a tree, old man," scoffed one of the older boys. "It doesn't whisper."

Zenji gently sat them down in the shade of the willow and began, "This tree, like all of nature, has stories to tell. Stories of resilience, hope, and life. Just because they are not voiced in words does not mean they aren't spoken. Every stretch of its bark, every flutter of its leaf, speaks of its journey. By harming it, you aren't just cutting off a branch; you're silencing a tale." He continued, "The willow does not resist the challenges; it adapts. It doesn't grow angry at the sky for lack of rain; it seeks moisture from deeper within the earth. In every challenge it faces, it finds an opportunity to grow, to evolve. That's its whisper, its lesson for all of us. Instead of resorting to myths, let us learn resilience from this very tree."

The children, now engrossed, listened intently. The older boy, feeling remorseful, said, "But what can we do, Zenji? Our crops are failing, and the river is drying." Zenji, with a twinkle in his eye, replied, "Remember the lesson of the willow. Adapt and find a way. Perhaps, the village can come together, dig deeper wells, store water better, or even seek new farming methods. Challenges are but nature's way of whispering lessons of resilience to us."

The children left, their perspectives altered. Word of Zenji's wisdom spread throughout the village. Over the following weeks, villagers united, implementing new water conservation methods, introducing drought-resistant crops, and sharing resources. The drought eventually passed, and the village flourished once more. But the real transformation was in the hearts of the villagers. They had learned the value of resilience, adaptability, and unity.

Zenji's daily visits to the willow continued. However, now he was often accompanied by villagers, young and old, who came not just to marvel at the tree's beauty but to listen, to hear the whispered tales of resilience it told. And thus, by the riverbank, under the shade of the enduring willow, a village learned to dance with challenges, always adapting, always resilient, always listening to the whispers of wisdom around them.

Of Bamboo and Storms:
Lessons in Bending, Not Breaking

*I*n the heart of an ancient village nestled high up in the misty mountains, there lived a venerable Zen monk named Zenshin, known throughout the land for his wisdom and tranquility. Zenshin spent many of his days tending to a grove of bamboo that grew beside his humble dwelling. The villagers often marveled at the meticulous care he extended towards these towering plants, nurturing them from the crack of dawn until the last light of dusk, in every season.

One particular afternoon, an impending storm began to brew at the distant horizon. The villagers scurried away to take cover, closing the shutters tightly and securing their homes against the assaulting wind. Zenshin, however, calmly continued his chores in the bamboo grove, his figure a quiet silhouette against the darkening sky. The storm rolled in with vehement fury. The mountains echoed with the tumultuous mixture of thunder and the furious howling wind. Yet, in the center of all this pandemonium, Zenshin remained with his bamboo, his composure as steadfast as the towering mountain itself.

In the heart of the tempest, the bamboo grove was a spectacle to behold. The wind whipped the tall bamboo stalks wildly, bending them to an almost impossible angle. Yet, they did not break. They swayed and danced, moving in tune with the ruthless storm's symphony. Amidst this spectacle, the monk appeared as a tranquil conductor, orchestrating a performance of resilience against the fierce forces of nature. From their safe havens, the villagers watched this spectacle with a mixture of terror and awe. Many feared for the old monk's safety, yet none dared to step out into the relentless storm. They could only watch as Zenshin and the bamboo danced in harmony with the storm, a display of calm acceptance in the face of adverse conditions.

As the day slipped into a stormy night, Zenshin's figure disappeared into the darkness, leaving the bamboo to face the fury of the storm. The villagers waited, their hearts filled with apprehension, wondering what lessons the monk and his bamboo would offer come the light of dawn. The morning light crept over the mountains, the storm a specter of the past, leaving in its wake a landscape draped in dew and silence. The villagers peeked out of their doors, their faces etched with concern, their gazes quickly turning towards the bamboo grove.

What met their eyes was a spectacle of resilience and strength. The bamboo grove stood tall, each stalk unbroken, their elegant curves testament to their battle with the storm. They held their heads high, a picture of graceful endurance, their leaves whispering tales of survival. In the midst of this scene, there emerged a figure, serenely making his way through the bamboo stalks. It was Zenshin, the corners of his eyes crinkling in a smile, his spirit undeterred by the storm's rage. In one hand, he held a bamboo stalk gently, its curve tracing the journey of resilience it had experienced. The villagers watched, their hearts awash with fresh understanding. The storm had been merciless, and yet, the bamboo had not broken. Instead, it had bent, danced, and swayed, moving in harmony with the storm rather than resisting it. It was a lesson in resilience and acceptance, a testament to the art of bending, not breaking.

Zenshin's voice echoed through the morning air, addressing the villagers. "Just as the bamboo bends with the storm but does not break, so must we learn to adapt and remain flexible with the storms of our lives. We cannot prevent storms, but we can choose how we respond. Dance with them, bend, but do not break." In the heart of their ancient village, under the watchful eyes of the resilient bamboo and the wise monk, the villagers promised to carry this lesson in their hearts. They would remember the dance of the bamboo in the storm, a symbol of strength, resilience, and the wisdom of bending, not breaking.

3

Stone's Quiet Dialogue with the Sculptor: Patience Perfected

Once upon a time, nestled on the edge of a quiet village, a solitary Zen monk named Kuzan made his abode. He was known throughout the land for his profound wisdom and his intriguing companionship with nature. His closest companion was a gargantuan, mute stone that rested peacefully beside the gurgling brook adjacent to his simple hut. Kuzan brought the stone home from the mountains during one of his solitary retreats, drawn to its uncut, rough beauty. The villagers were intrigued by this unusual friendship. They couldn't help but wonder why a man of such enlightenment and wisdom invested so much time and affection in a mere stone. But Kuzan knew his companion was far from ordinary. He saw a spirit trapped within the stone, yearning to be set free.

One day, Kuzan picked up a sculptor's chisel and began to work on freeing the hidden form within the stone. The villagers watched in silent bewilderment as day after day, under the shade of the old banyan tree, the monk gently chipped away at the stone. Kuzan worked with a patience that was both nurturing and relentless. Each tap of the chisel was a dialogue between him and the stone. He listened to its whispers and responded with a gentle touch, always careful not to force his desires upon the stone.

Weeks turned into months, and the seasons changed around them, but Kuzan's commitment did not waver. Winter rains washed the stone, summer sun dried it, and autumn winds swept the leaves around it, yet the monk tirelessly continued his endeavor. Villagers passing by would stop to observe the transformation. The raw, uncut stone was slowly revealing a form, a shape was beginning to emerge, reflecting the silent dialogue between the Zen monk and his stone companion. Yet, what it would become was still a mystery. Their curiosity piqued, they returned home each day, wondering about the outcome of the Zen monk's patient endeavor.

As the second winter began to blanket the village, the figure within the stone began to take a recognizable form. The villagers, bundled in their winter attire, stopped frequently beside the banyan tree, their eyes filled with wonder as they looked upon the emerging sculpture. It was a reflection of Kuzan himself, sitting in a meditative pose, the essence of tranquility captured flawlessly in stone. Yet, Kuzan's work was far from over. More months passed, the chisel continuing its dialogue with the stone, drawing out not just the physical likeness but also the spiritual essence of the meditating monk. Kuzan's patience was not just about crafting the sculpture, but also about allowing the stone to reveal its deepest secrets and transform at its own pace. The villagers marveled at the monk's unwavering patience. Some even began to understand that Kuzan's relationship with the stone was not about possession or creation, but about co-existence and mutual transformation. They saw that the stone was not merely yielding to Kuzan's chisel, but also subtly shaping the monk in return.

The day finally came when the last chip was carved, and Kuzan set his chisel down. The stone, now a mirror image of Kuzan in meditative serenity, was silent. The dialogue was over. The villagers gathered around, their faces glowing with admiration, their hearts resonating with a profound, shared wisdom. Kuzan looked at his stone companion and smiled. For him, the sculpture was a testament not to his skill or artistry, but to the stone's quiet endurance and patience. He had not created something new, but merely helped reveal what was always there. Through the stone, Kuzan had demonstrated the power of patience, the possibility of transformation, and the blossoming wisdom that comes from a silent dialogue with the world around us.

4

Whispering Pine's Guidance: Leading the Lost Home

As the morning rays of the sun, soft and warm, caressed the sleepy valley, the Zen Monk began his journey. His destination was not a geographical spot, but a point of inner awakening. Covered in a simple yellow robe, a bamboo staff in hand, he walked with a soulful grace through the lush emerald forest. He walked gently on the moss-covered earth. With every step, he acknowledged the life beneath him, extending his thanks to the rocks for their patience, the roots for their silent endurance, and the earth for her nurturing love. He heard the symphony of the forest - the rustle of leaves, the melody of the birds, the whispering winds, the rhythmic breathing of the towering trees.

Among them all, a majestic pine tree caught his attention. It stood tall and solitary, like a sage in deep Samadhi. Its needle-like green leaves, coupled with the soothing scent of its bark, seemed to whisper tales of wisdom. The Monk was drawn towards it, a moth to a flame. He rested his worn-out body against the rugged trunk, feeling the pulse of the ancient tree, its silent strength, its stories of endurance.

Suddenly, he noticed a small bird circling above him, fluttering its wings in a frenzy. The bird seemed lost, away from its nest, struggling with the wind currents. The Monk watched the creature's plight, his heart swelling with compassion. His gaze then fell upon the towering pine, standing tall as if reaching out to the lost bird, guiding it towards its sanctuary. His heart sought solace in the tree's quiet wisdom. Like the bird, he too was on a journey home - not towards a physical dwelling, but a state of inner peace, a reunion with his true self. He could sense the tree's guidance in his journey, subtle yet profound, leading him home.

The Monk closed his eyes, allowing himself to become one with the whispering pine, its nurturing shadow cloaking him with a sense of reassurance and acceptance. Even without words, the pine had begun to guide him, silently and gently leading the lost soul home.

As he leaned against the whispering pine, the Monk sensed a shift in his consciousness, a silent communication with the world around him. The concerns of his spirit turned lighter, and he felt the steady rhythm of the pine's life energy mingling with his own.

The tiny bird, still whirling in the sky, seemed to tune into this silent exchange. It slowly and hesitantly began to arc towards the tree, following an invisible path etched by the pine's silent guidance. Its flight became less frantic, more purposeful, till it finally found its way to a nest cradled in the sturdy arms of the pine. The Monk opened his eyes just as the bird nestled comfortably into its home. A gentle smile spread across his face. He recognized this moment as an echo of his own journey. Like the bird, he too was slowly but surely moving towards his destination - a destination not marked on any map, but rather in the depths of his consciousness.

Drawing strength and wisdom from the whispering pine, the Monk continued his journey, his spirit lighter, his path clearer. The forest, in its infinite wisdom, had shown him that sometimes, the guidance we seek is not in the form of loud pronouncements, but in the subtle whispers of nature. As the sun set, painting the sky in hues of red and gold, the Monk felt an inner sunrise. He realized that he was not lost, but simply on his way. This journey was not just about reaching a destination, but also about understanding the transitions, the winding paths, and the silent guides along the way. Embracing this wisdom, the Monk stepped forward. For he now knew, like the bird, he would find his way home, guided by the whispering pines and his blossoming wisdom.

5

The Stream's Melody to the Boulder: Fluidity Over Force

In a tranquil valley, nestled between the earth's giant shoulders, there flowed a cherry stream. Her soothing voice echoed through the rocks and woods, a gentle lullaby to all creatures of the valley. The stream, despite her gentle nature, held a determined purpose - a journey to reach the grand ocean. Along her path sat an imposing boulder, unyielding and stern. No wind or weather had ever managed to shift it an inch, and the stream's way was blocked. The boulder, with its stubborn might and substantial size, seemed an insurmountable obstacle. The stream, however, did not fret over the obstacle. She caressed the boulder, seeping into its crevices, softly whispering her song into its hard surface. Yet, the boulder remained unmoved, standing like an indomitable wall between the stream and her destination.

One day, a wandering Zen Monk found his way into the magical valley. He had heard the valley's tales from fellow wanderers, of its tranquil stream, the stubborn boulder, and their never-ending dance. Intrigued, he chose to rest by the stream and observe her constant interaction with the boulder. The monk watched the stream as she flowed, her gentle ripples lapping against the boulder in a persistent rhythm. Her melody, rich with determination and patience, filled the air with an enchanting tune. He noticed the way the stream continued to embrace the boulder, seemingly unperturbed by its refusal to budge. A sense of calm serenity enveloped the monk as he observed, the stream's melody lulling him into contemplation.

The sun moved in its arc, casting a cascade of colors into the sky as day rolled into twilight. The valley, bathed in the soft glow of the setting sun, seemed to hold its breath, its usual cacophony hushed to respect the stream's melody.

The night blanketed the valley, the moon casting silver hues across the landscape. But the stream, she never ceased her melody, continuing her soft whisper to the stubborn boulder. Time seemed to stretch, the rhythm unwavering, a testament to her unwavering resolve and the grace of her fluidity. As dawn broke, splashing hues of gold and crimson across the valley, the monk was stirred from his contemplation by a subtle shift — a harmony he had not noticed before. The boulder, the immovable boulder, showed signs of change. To a casual eye, it would be all but unnoticeable, but the monk, in his focused observation, could see it. The boulder had begun to yield to the stream's gentle persuasion.

Across its rough surface, the sound of the stream echoed a little louder, and tiny rivulets were forming, seeping deeper into the boulder's crevices. The boulder was slowly, imperceptibly, but definitely, wearing away under the delicate touch of the stream. The monk's heart warmed at the sight. He saw wisdom in the stream's approach - it was not through force, rage, or violence that she sought her path, but through persistence, grace, and the fluidity of her embrace. She did not seek to conquer the boulder but instead aimed to coexist, to meld with it, to mold it through persistent and patient love.

The boulder, too, in its stern obstinacy, held a lesson. It was not invincible, nor immovable. It was merely waiting for the right force to touch it - gentle, loving, and persistent. The boulder, though seemingly stubborn, was slowly accepting the stream, allowing her to carve her path and continue her journey without losing its own form. Rather, it was becoming a part of her journey, a supporting role in her quest. The monk rose, a soft smile etched on his serene face. The valley had shared its wisdom - about fluidity, patience, and the power of gentle persistence. As he moved on, he took the melody of the stream and the whisper of the boulder in his heart, a gentle reminder of wisdom found in the rhythm of nature, in the dance of the stream and the boulder.

6

Climber's Pursuit of Peaks: The Passion to Rise Above

*I*n a small village at the foot of the majestic Himalayas, lived a young man named Tenzin. The mountains, standing tall and unyielding, had always fascinated him. The villagers often joked about how Tenzin would watch the snowy peaks as a child, his eyes wide with awe and his heart brimming with a passion that was as profound as it was inexplicable. As Tenzin aged, his fascination turned into a zeal that was impossible to quench. He was often found meandering on the thresholds of the mountains, feeling the icy winds against his face, embracing the chill that seeped into his bones, and absorbing the silence that seemed to echo his innermost desires. It was as if the mountains were his sanctuary and the race to the top was his soul's pursuit.

One day, as the sun painted the sky with hues of gold and crimson, Tenzin announced to his fellow villagers his intention to conquer the highest peak of the Himalayas, the mighty Everest. The villagers gaped at him, their faces mirroring a blend of astonishment and concern. They knew the mountains could be unforgiving, their beauty hiding a multitude of challenges. Despite their worries, Tenzin was steadfast. His face was a picture of tranquil determination and his eyes sparkled with a zest that was contagious. He wasn't merely attracted to the idea of standing at the world's highest point; rather, it was the journey that intrigued him. For him, every difficulty was a riddle to be solved, every stumble a lesson to be learned, and every moment an opportunity for self-discovery.

The climb was going to be arduous, a journey that would test his strength, patience, and courage. He understood this fully. And as he packed his bag, with every piece of gear meticulously chosen and every ration thoughtfully packed, he knew that this was not just a physical expedition but a voyage into the depths of his own spirit. He was ready to heed the call of the mountains, to rise above the mundane and embrace the extraordinary.

The day had come for Tenzin to undertake his challenging journey. With prayer flags tied around his waist as a token of blessings from his folks, he set off towards the mountain with a heart throbbing with anticipation. He knew the path would be daunting, laden with crevasses, treacherous icefalls, and precarious ledges. But the mountains had instilled in him a fearlessness that resonated with every beat of his heart.

With every arduous step, Tenzin felt more connected to the mountain. He became an integral part of the open sky, the fierce wind, and the unyielding icy peaks. He spoke to the mountain with every breath, every exertion, every bead of sweat, and the mountain answered through the crunch of the snow beneath his boots and the hollow echo of the wilderness. The ascent was grueling, but Tenzin relished the hardship. Every muscle strain was a sign of his growing strength, every gust of wind a test of his resilience, every progress a testament to his undying passion. There were moments of despair, moments when his body wailed in protest, moments when the enormity of his endeavor loomed over him like a dark cloud. But he remained undeterred.

After days of climbing, Tenzin stood atop the highest peak in the world. His heart pounded with triumphant joy, but there was a calmness within him that was as colossal as the peak beneath his feet. He gazed at the world beneath him, the houses, the village, now mere specks in the vast landscape, and realized how he had risen above the mundane, to embrace a life of purposeful passion.

His journey was not just about conquering the highest peak; it was about conquering his self-doubt, his fears, and his limitations. He had indeed reached the peak, but he had discovered much more – his blossoming wisdom. And with this newfound wisdom, he was ready to conquer not just mountains, but life.

7

Mysteries in Tea Leaves: Embracing Life's Fleeting Moments

On a brisk, spring morning in the serene Kyoto Gardens, the Zen Monk sat under an ancient, blossoming cherry blossom tree. Before him, a humble bamboo tea tray held a small, darkened teapot along with two dainty cups. A steaming pot of water sat nearby. Beneath the swirling colors of the dawn, a young disciple named Kenta, a newcomer to the monastery, approached the monk with apprehension. He was unsure of his place in this world of quiet reflection and sacred rituals.

"Master," Kenta bowed respectfully and sat across from the monk on the cushioned mat. The monk returned the bow with a gentle nod, a hint of a smile on his lips. He pointed Kenta towards the teapot with a directive to serve, a part of the monastery's morning tea ritual. With hesitant hands, Kenta reached out for the small, darkened teapot, his fingers brushing over the intricately carved patterns. He watched as the dark green tea swirled in the pot, like a tiny storm brewing under the surface. He served tea in both cups, the warm liquid pouring out with a gentle, hissing sound that echoed the calm of the garden around them.

The monk lifted his cup delicately, bringing it to his lips with a reverence that made Kenta hold his breath. He observed as the monk took a deep sip, closing his eyes as if savoring every molecule of the brew. Kenta followed suit, his lips meeting the rim of the cup, the warmth spreading through his body, calming his racing heart. Setting his cup aside, the monk gestured towards the tiny leaves that had settled at the bottom of his cup. His eyes twinkled with an unspoken mystery as he slid the cup across to the young disciple.

Kenta peered into the cup, perplexed. He saw irregular shapes and outlines, scattered in a chaotic array...or maybe they were patterns? His mind whirred with questions he dared not voice, his gaze fixed upon the monk. He was to learn, after all, and the day had only begun.

The monk's soft eyes met Kenta's questioning gaze. "What do you see, Kenta?" he asked, his voice barely above a whisper, as if afraid to disturb the harmony of the garden.

"Leaves, Master." Kenta replied hesitantly. "Just tea leaves." The monk chuckled gently, a warm sound that matched the soothing tones of the morning sun. "Yes, they are tea leaves. Yet, in them, lie answers. The ways of the universe are revealed, in the smallest of things, if we only take the time to truly see."

Puzzled, Kenta stared again into the cup. No longer did he see just leaves, but the shapes they formed. He saw a mountain, a river, a blossoming tree, all things he loved, all things he was. His heart swelled with a warmth that spread through his veins like the tea he'd consumed. "The tea offers us a glimpse into the fleeting nature of our lives, Kenta," the monk continued. "Just as these leaves alter their form and purpose, so do we. Embrace the changes, for they are the essence of life."

Kenta looked back at the monk, his eyes now wide with wonder. He looked again towards the cup, his heart resonating with the monk's wisdom. The mystery in the tea leaves had begun to unravel, and with it, the complexities of his own existence. His apprehension had dissolved into acceptance, his uncertainty into understanding. The world of quiet reflection and sacred rituals no longer seemed alien. He was ready for the journey, ready to conquer the unchartered territories of his mind, ready to find his place in the grand scheme of existence. The Zen monk smiled at his young disciple, his eyes reflecting the serenity of the dawn. Kenta had taken his first step towards wisdom. The day indeed had just begun.

8

Cloud's Journey with the Mountain: Accepting the Unmovable

Once upon a time, in a world where nature breathed tales of wisdom and introspection, there lived an ambitious little cloud named Nimbus. Nimbus was cherished by the sky for his lively spirit and boundless curiosity. Yet, there was one thing that puzzled and frustrated Nimbus - the immovable mountain, Everest. Unlike his cloud companions who chose to float and frolic with the wind, Nimbus, who was filled with youthful vigor and a thirst for understanding, found himself drawn to Everest. Why is it that he, a cloud, could dance with the winds, while Everest stood rooted like an ancient sage? Nimbus began his journey toward the mountain, fueled by the desire to comprehend the essence of this eternal stillness.

Taking it upon himself to comprehend the immovable, Nimbus made his way towards Everest. As he sailed closer, the mountain's majesty and quiet power took his breath away. Everest stood there, unmoved by the elements, its peak adorned with a crown of snow, and its body draped in a shroud of green. It was steadfast, resolute, and patient, a silent testament to time and its unfolding narrative. From his ephemeral home up in the sky, Nimbus began conversing with the mountain. "Everest," Nimbus asked, "Why is it that you don't move like us clouds? Why do you choose to remain rooted in one place?"

Everest, in his quiet wisdom, didn't respond. The mountain's silence struck Nimbus, leaving him feel both frustrated and awestruck.

But undeterred, he came back each day, asking his questions and seeking the truths of stillness. Nimbus continued to live between the earth and the sky, oscillating between his soft, flowing nature and his yearning to understand the steady, unmoving mountain. Unbeknownst to him, this continual journey was leading him towards a profound lesson he was yet to uncover. Days turned into weeks, and weeks into months. Nimbus kept returning to Everest with the same curiosity, the same questions. Each time, he found the mountain in the same grand state of unmoving silence. And each time, Nimbus left with a heavy heart, pondering upon the mystery that was Everest.

One day, as Nimbus was engaged in his usual quest, a powerful gust of wind came along, carrying him far away from Everest. Nimbus struggled and resisted, but the wind's force was too mighty. It pushed him over deserts, oceans, and cities, but no matter how far he was taken, Nimbus never lost sight of Everest. In his relentless journey, Nimbus saw the ebbs and flows of life on earth. He saw seasons change, civilizations rise and fall, children grow into adults, and seeds turn into mighty trees. Yet through it all, even from a distance, he saw Everest standing tall, undeterred, unchanging.

A realization washed over Nimbus. As a cloud, he was destined to flow and roam, to see the world and its transient nature. Everest's role, however, was different. The mountain stood firm as a beacon of constancy amidst the fluidity of life, a symbol of stability in an ever-changing world. By being immovable, Everest was not missing out on the dance of life. It was, in its own way, participating in the grand spectacle, illustrating the omnipresence of eternity amidst change. Nimbus realized that both he, the ever-moving cloud, and Everest, the unflinching mountain, had their unique places in the tapestry of existence. From then on, Nimbus carried this wisdom in his heart, a newfound respect for Everest in his soul, and a sense of inner peace. His journey for understanding had indeed led him to an unexpected destination - the blossoming of wisdom within himself.

Buddha's Smile, Child's Tears:
Balancing Joy and Sorrow

Once upon a time, in a small village nestled between emerald mountains and a river that hummed with secrets, there lived an ancient Zen Monk named Kōhō. He was known far and wide for his sage-like wisdom and the tranquility that seemed to radiate from his very being. As it was, a young boy from the village, Kaito, was taken by his mother to Kōhō's humble dwelling. Kaito's eyes were brimming with tears, his heart heavy with sorrow. His lips trembled as he recounted the pain of losing his beloved pet, a small, sprightly rabbit that had been his most steadfast companion.

Kōhō, in his woven straw hat, listened calmly, his eyes closed. The morning sun, peeking through the temple's rustic wooden lattices, caressed his weathered face, revealing lines of wisdom etched deep and folds of kindness that marked his years. As the boy wept, pouring out his anguish to the old monk, Kōhō simply sat in silence. His eyes, when opened, revealed depths of understanding that seemed to encompass the entire universe. His hands, gnarled and weathered, held a beautifully blossoming cherry twig that he was carefully tending to.

Suddenly, as if sensing the boy's despair, the monk reached out, and with a soft touch, wiped the cascading tears from Kaito's face. Then, as if conjuring a moment of pure serenity, he broke into a heartwarming smile. It was said that Kōhō's smile could make flowers bloom and even the darkest storm clouds part. This simple gesture, this Buddha's smile, seemed to reach into Kaito's depths, and for a fleeting moment, his sobbing ceased, his heart stilled. Yet, the tears soon welled up again, as if the loss he felt was a deep wound, fresh and raw.

Kōhō, however, continued to smile, radiating peace and calm, while carefully tending to the cherry twig, as if balancing the boy's sorrow with his tranquil joy. Kōhō, gently placing the cherry twig aside, took a deep breath. His eyes, mirroring the vastness of the skies, met Kaito's tear-filled ones. As the young boy's sobs filled the quiet morning, Kōhō calmly asked, "Kaito, why do you think this cherry twig blooms with such beauty?" Kaito, his face wet with tears, looked at the cherry twig. Through his blurred eyes, he could see the vibrant flowers standing radiant against the lush green leaves. He wiped his tears and whispered, "I do not know, Kōhō-sama."

Kōhō, his smile deepening, looked at the cherry twig, and then back at Kaito. He gently said, "The cherry blossom endures the bitter cold winter, waiting in silent patience. It withstands the harsh winds, the biting frost, and the deep snow. Yet, it does not lose faith. It knows that spring will arrive, and with it, the warmth of the sun. Only then does it bloom, radiating beauty and joy. The sorrow of winter and the joy of spring, the cherry blossom embraces both." Kaito listened, his tears slowing, his heart quieting. He looked at the cherry twig, his grief-stricken eyes now filled with a glimmer of understanding. Kōhō, in the same calm voice, continued, "Life, Kaito, is a blend of joy and sorrow. You must allow your heart to feel the pain, just as the cherry blossom endures the winter. But remember, like the cherry blossom, your heart too will bloom, when the time is right."

With this, Kōhō handed the twig to Kaito. As the young boy clutched the twig, he felt a sense of calm wash over him. The tears ceased, his heart, though heavy, began to steady. As he looked at Kōhō, the monk's smile seemed even warmer, his wisdom, even deeper. Kaito understood. Life, like the cherry blossom, was a balance of sorrow and joy. Embracing both was the path to wisdom and tranquility.

10

Mirrors in the Pond: Discovering Authenticity

𝓘n a serene corner of Japan, nestled amidst the churning seas and ancient mountains, lay a tranquil monastery. Here, an old Zen monk named Tetsuo lived, renowned for his wisdom and revered by many. Invoked by his reputation, a troubled young samurai named Hiroshi sought him out one sunny afternoon.

"Master Tetsuo," Hiroshi began, kneeling respectfully before the monk, "my life is plagued by restlessness. I find myself donning a different mask for every person I meet. It's as if I'm a mere reflection of their expectations, not truly myself." His eyes, weary and clouded, desperately pleaded for guidance. The monk, his face etched with lines of wisdom and eyes sparkling with discernment, nodded understandingly. He invited Hiroshi to follow him on a walk through the lush garden surrounding the monastery. The sweet scent of cherry blossoms filled the air, adding a sense of serenity to their journey. As they strolled across the verdant expanse, Tetsuo led the young samurai to a crystal-clear pond. The pond was a mirror, reflecting the vibrancy of the sky above and the surrounding flora in exquisite detail. The echo of koi fish splashing and the whispers of rustling leaves served as a gentle symphony to the spectacle.

"Look at the pond, Hiroshi," Tetsuo commanded, his voice echoing the tranquility around them. Hiroshi obeyed, gazing into the glassy surface of the water, observing his own image reflecting back at him. The monk's aged hand reached out, sending a ripple through the water. A disturbed reflection stared back at Hiroshi, morphing and fluctuating with every ripple until it finally settled once more. The samurai looked at the monk, puzzled. A knowing smile stretched across Tetsuo's face.

"The lesson isn't complete yet, Hiroshi. Come, let us walk further," Tetsuo suggested, his staff tapping rhythmically against the stone pathway as they moved away from the pond. As Hiroshi followed, his mind buzzed with silent thoughts, curiosity piqued, awaiting the layers of wisdom that were yet to be unfolded. They walked in silence, the rustle of leaves and the tranquil hum of nature filling the brief pause in their conversation. After a while, they reached a grove of cherry blossom trees, the ground beneath speckled with soft pink petals. Tetsuo stopped and gently picked up a fallen blossom, handling it with a reverence that drew Hiroshi's attention.

"This blossom," Tetsuo said, holding it for Hiroshi to see, "is undeniably itself, no matter where it lands. Even if it falls into the pond and its reflection is distorted by the ripples, it remains a cherry blossom. It doesn't change to match the expectations of the wind or the pond." Hiroshi listened, his brows knitted in deep thought. Tetsuo continued this analogy, "You, Hiroshi, are like this blossom. The world is the pond, with its constant ripples of expectations and judgments. Your reflection may change in the eyes of others, but that does not change who you truly are."

Hiroshi looked from the blossom to Tetsuo, a spark of understanding dancing in his eyes. The monk, satisfied that the young samurai was grasping the essence of his teaching, released the blossom. It floated down, landing on the surface of the pond, its reflection visible amongst the ripples. "Your task, Hiroshi," Tetsuo concluded as they began their walk back to the monastery, "is not to resist the ripples, but to recognize and remain true to your own authentic self amidst them." Hiroshi nodded, the burden of his restlessness feeling slightly lighter. The wisdom of the monk, like the echo of the koi fish in the pond and the whispering leaves, lingered in his mind, encouraging him on his path towards discovering authenticity.

11

Firefly's Beacon in Darkness: Finding Light Within

*I*n the quiet town of Sanyu, nestled in the arms of ancient mountains, there lived an old Zen monk, Shodo. Every dusk, Shodo would sit in his humble garden, enjoying the peaceful symphony of nature while sipping his warm tea. He lived in a simple cottage, adorned with cherry blossom trees that whispered tales of wisdom to those that dared to listen. Shodo was known far and wide for his peaceful demeanor, his tranquil wisdom, and his knack for creating joy out of simplicity. Many sought Shodo's teachings, yet it was not his words that enlightened but rather, his silent actions which spoke volumes.

One dusky evening, a young boy from the village, Ichiro, found his way to Shodo's quaint garden. It was a difficult time for Ichiro. His mother had fallen ill, his father worked tirelessly to make ends meet, and he felt a profound darkness clouding his heart. The world he once knew was crumbling, and he was lost in a maze of despair. He had heard of the wise Shodo, of his tranquil aura that somehow made everything seem better, and he sought refuge in the monk's wisdom. As Ichiro entered the garden, he found Shodo sitting under a cherry blossom tree, his eyes closed in deep meditation, his serene face illuminated by the dying embers of the sun. The garden was barely lit, save for the twinkle of fireflies that danced around the Zen monk like tiny, glowing fairies. Ichiro observed Shodo, his calmness, the peaceful aura that surrounded him, and the soft glow of the fireflies in the dim light. He noticed the delicate nature of those fireflies, their light so soft and yet so illuminating in the darkness.

It was then that Ichiro realized that even in the profound depths of darkness, light could be found - like the fireflies, shining amidst the gloom. Intrigued and comforted by this realization, he approached Shodo, eager to learn more. As Ichiro approached, Shodo opened his eyes. He looked at the boy, his gaze kind and understanding, as if he could see the turmoil within him. "You seem troubled, young Ichiro," the monk said, his voice as soothing as the rustling leaves of the trees. The boy was taken aback, wondering how the monk knew his name. "People and their stories aren't much different from our fireflies," Shodo continued, "Each carrying unique light within, some brighter, some dimmer."

Ichiro, his curiosity piqued, asked, "But Master Shodo, what if the light within us flickers and dies? How do we shine then?" Shodo smiled and pointed at the fireflies. "Look at them, Ichiro," he said. "Some are brighter than others, yet they all shine. Not despite the darkness, but because of it. Their light doesn't die; it only seems dimmer when surrounded by other brightness. The light within us is similar." Ichiro pondered the wisdom in Shodo's words. The monk continued, "Life has a way of dimming our light sometimes, making us feel lost. But remember, the firefly's light shines the brightest in the darkest of nights. Similarly, our inner light shines in the face of adversity, guiding us, comforting us."

The boy looked at the fireflies, their glow seemed brighter, their dance more joyous. He felt lighter, the darkness in his heart easing. He understood that he held a beacon within himself, a light to guide him through his troubles. That night, he walked back home, his steps lighter, his heart hopeful. In the darkness, he had found his inner firefly, and he knew it would guide him just as the fireflies guided Shodo in his peaceful garden. Now, he was eager to share this newfound wisdom with his family, to help them find their inner fireflies too.

12

Ant's Triumph Over the Leaf: Celebrating Small Victories

O nce upon a time, nestled amidst the towering blades of grass in a vast garden, lived an ant named Miro. Miro was not extraordinary by ant standards, neither the strongest nor the swiftest among his peers. He was, however, a diligent worker, steadfast in his purpose. One dewy morning, Miro was assigned to transport a fallen leaf back to their anthill. At first glance, the leaf, golden and glistening in the morning sunlight, appeared almost majestic. But for Miro, it was a colossal challenge, a giant relic of the trees towering above, almost thrice his size. Yet, this was his duty, and he was determined to accomplish it.

Miro approached the leaf with trepidation, his antennae quivering. He surveyed the best way to navigate the leaf's size and was soon hard at work. With each passing moment, Miro struggled, pushing and pulling, his tiny legs straining under the weight. The task was undoubtedly arduous, and many times he faltered, losing his grip and tumbling down. Yet, he was undeterred. With each fall, he dusted himself off and returned to his task. At times, Miro felt the scorching sun overhead adding to his ordeal, and other times, chilled winds would counter his progress, threatening to blow away his precious cargo. At those moments, Miro would clench his jaws tighter, anchoring the leaf firmly to the earth.

His task was not without spectators. The other ants buzzed around in their tasks, often pausing to watch him struggle. Some snickered and whispered about how Miro would never surmount this challenge, while others simply watched in silent doubt. However,

Miro was undeterred by their skepticism. The daunting task before him was his responsibility, and he would not let the leaf, or the whispers of doubt, overcome him. With each step he took, with each small triumph of moving the leaf an inch closer to the anthill, Miro's determination only grew stronger. And the day wore on, with Miro's battle against the leaf unfolding under the vast sky.

As dusk approached, Miro felt his strength dwindling. His legs trembled with fatigue, and for the first time, doubt clouded his mind. He paused for a moment, gazing at the distant anthill that still seemed so far away. Just then, a gust of wind blew across the garden, rustling the blades of grass and nudging the leaf slightly forward. Miro watched as the leaf moved, and his tiny heart surged with a newfound determination. He was not alone in his struggle; even nature was aiding his cause. With renewed vigor, he charged at the leaf, pushing with all his might, inching it bit by bit towards the anthill.

The sun began to set, painting the sky with hues of orange and pink, and a cheer erupted from the onlooking ants. Miro had accomplished what had seemed impossible; he had moved the gargantuan leaf to the anthill. His perseverance and tenacity had won the day. Exhausted but triumphant, Miro stood atop the leaf, gazing across the now quiet garden. The whispers of the other ants had been replaced by whispers of admiration and awe. Even the elements seemed to be celebrating his victory, with the setting sun casting a golden glow around him.

And so, Miro, the average ant, had shown that no task is impossible when met with determination and hard work. He had not only conquered the leaf but also the negativity around him, discovering joy in his achievement. The day had started with a colossal challenge, and it ended with an even bigger triumph. From then on, Miro was no longer just an average ant. He had become a symbol of steadfastness and determination, a beacon of inspiration for the other ants, teaching them that every daunting task can be overcome with persistence and a positive outlook.

13

Maple's Autumnal Farewell: Embracing Seasonal Shifts

Once upon a time in the tranquil countryside of ancient Japan, lived a wise Zen monk named Tetsuo. He had a deep, spiritual connection with nature and considered the trees, the rivers, the birds as his own kin. Particularly, he was fond of an old maple tree that stood majestically near the monastery. The tree was older than the oldest monk in the monastery, its roots as deep as their traditions and its branches reaching out to the heavens, just like their prayers. Tetsuo talked to it, meditated under it, and sometimes even slept under it, lulled to sleep by the sound of rustling leaves dancing in the gentle breeze.

Autumn had arrived that year in full glory, painting the canvas of the monastery landscape with warm hues of red, orange, and gold. The old maple, now ablaze in the sunset of its life, was a spectacle to behold. Tetsuo, however, felt a strange melancholy. He was distressed by the thought of the tree shedding its leaves, standing barren and skeletal against the harsh winter to come. He dreaded the sight of his beloved maple stripped of its grandeur, its bare branches shivering in the cold.

One day, while meditating under the maple, an autumn leaf, with colors of a setting sun, fell gently into his lap. It was beautiful, yet its detachment from the tree brought a pang of sadness to his heart. He picked it up gently, tracing his fingers over the delicate veins that once carried life-sustaining nutrients. It was a poignant reminder of the inevitability of change - the relentless march of time that spares none. As the leaf crumbled in his hand, Tetsuo looked up to see more leaves preparing to take their final leap, to bid goodbye to their home of many sunny days and starlit nights. He knew he couldn't stop this cycle - after all, nature must take its course. But how to accept this change with grace? That was the question that stirred in Tetsuo's heart, as he watched the maple's autumnal farewell.

The following day, Tetsuo sat again under the maple, the ground now a rich tapestry of fallen leaves. He closed his eyes and connected with the quiet rhythm of nature, feeling the cool breeze whispering tales of change - tales of birth, growth, decay, and rebirth. He felt the tree's wisdom flow into him, its silent acceptance of nature's cycle filling him with an understanding he had been seeking. He understood that the tree was not grieving for the lost leaves. Rather, it was celebrating the transformation that was to come. The leaves had served their purpose, and now, just as monks learn to let go of worldly attachments, the tree was letting go of its leaves. It was not a tragedy, but a necessary passage leading to renewal. The bare branches did not signify the end, but a pause, a rest before the tree would burst into life again in the spring, rejuvenated and refreshed. The tree was not shivering in the winter cold but stood strong and resilient, braving the chill with courage and grace.

With this realization, Tetsuo felt a profound peace settle within him. His distress had transformed into a calm acceptance of the inevitability and beauty of change. He realized that life was not merely about holding on, but also about letting go when the time was right, about knowing when to let things fall away to make room for new growth. As he got up to leave, Tetsuo gently picked up a fallen leaf, not with a sense of loss, but with gratitude for the wisdom it had imparted. He looked at the old maple, standing tall and serene against the evening sky, and smiled. It was, indeed, a beautiful farewell, a promise of life continuing in an endless cycle, of letting go to embrace the new. And thus, Tetsuo learned to embrace the seasonal shifts of life, understanding that every ending is, in truth, a new beginning.

14

Songbird's Serenade for the Quiet Monk: Listening to Life's Melodies

A gentle breeze rustled the towering bamboo trees. Their leaves danced rhythmically to the songs of the universe. In the midst of this serene forest, nestled on the mountainside, was a modest monastery. A place where silence itself was a beloved companion. Here, a Zen monk, known for his unwavering tranquility, lived a life devoted to reflection and wisdom. The monk, who the villagers delightfully referred to as Brother Serenity, was a beacon of calm and inspiration.

On this specific day, the sun had risen, casting a kaleidoscope of colors across the horizon. As Brother Serenity sat in his usual meditative stance in the monastery's garden, he noticed a new entrant - a humble songbird. The bird perched itself on a nearby cherry blossom tree, unbothered by the presence of the monk. Its feathers were a radiant mosaic, quite unlike anything he had ever seen, reflecting colors with an almost otherworldly luster. The songbird began its serenade, its melody serene and enchanting. Brother Serenity's sensitive ears, trained by years of deep silence, could pick up every note, every trill, every tiny inflection in the bird's voice. It was as if, through its song, the bird was narrating tales of distant lands, of moonlit oceans, of storms weathered and of love discovered.

As the songbird continued its serenade, Brother Serenity closed his eyes. There was something about this simple act of nature that stirred something in him. He was reminded of an ancient Zen saying, "In the silence, there is eloquence." But why had the saying come to mind now? The songbird's melody was certainly not silence. Or was it? The monk pondered over this thought. He knew that the answers he sought were not hidden in some ancient text or philosophical discourse, but were there in the melody of the songbird, in the breeze rustling the bamboo trees, in the scent of the blossoming cherry blossoms.

And so, Brother Serenity listened, a warm smile on his face as he welcomed the serenade of life. Days turned into weeks and the songbird continued to visit each morning. Its melodies became the soundtrack to Brother Serenity's meditations and contemplations, a harmonious mix, blending with the ambient sounds of nature. Each day, he heard a new tale in the bird's song - stories of endurance, of resilience, of the quiet trust in the cycles of life and seasons.

Then, one day, the songbird did not come. The forest seemed to hold its breath in the absence of the bird's music. Brother Serenity felt the silence, deeper and more profound than before. The ancient Zen saying echoed in his mind again, "In the silence, there is eloquence." And in that moment, the monk understood. He realized that it was not silence against noise but silence amidst noise. It was a silence of peace, of acceptance, of simply being. The songbird's melody, the rustling of the bamboo leaves, the blooming of the cherry blossoms were all a part of this eloquent silence. Each was performing its role in the symphony of life, contributing to its harmony.

When the songbird returned the next day, Brother Serenity greeted it with a warmed heart. The bird's melody was indeed not silence, but it was a part of the eloquence that silence held. It was in the acceptance of these concerts of life's sounds that one could find tranquility, the tranquility that the monk had always known. The songbird, with its vibrant colors and enchanting melodies, had indeed brought a new understanding to Brother Serenity, an understanding of listening, of being, and of embracing the rhythms of life. And the Zen monk, in his quiet and contemplative way, had discovered a new layer of wisdom in the humble songbird's serenade. In listening, he had understood, and in understanding, he had found a deeper peace.

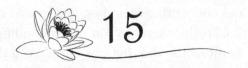

15

Boat's Peaceful Voyage on Still Waters: The Calm of Letting Be

*T*here once lived a grand Zen monk, Master Gensho, of profound wisdom and serene countenance, in the outskirts of the ancient town of Zenkoji. Nestled among mighty mountains and sacred streams, the town was a quiet refuge for the wandering souls. Master Gensho's tranquil personality and profound wisdom drew many seekers of wisdom and peace from far and wide. One early morning, when the sun was just beginning to peek through the misty clouds, a young merchant, Takeshi, arrived at the doorstep of Master Gensho's humble dwelling. Takeshi was a successful trade merchant who, despite his prosperity, was distraught by constant worry, stress, and a sense of unfulfillment. He had heard of the Zen monk's wisdom and hoped to find answers that eluded him, solutions to calm his restless mind. Master Gensho welcomed Takeshi and listened to his troubles. After a long pause filled with silence, Master Gensho suggested, "Come, let us take a journey."

Without explaining further, Master Gensho led Takeshi to a beautiful wooden boat he had crafted with his own hands, resting serenely on a still lake adjacent to his dwelling. As the day was just breaking, the surroundings were bathed in an ethereal glow and the still waters mirrored the tranquil beauty of the morning. Master Gensho gestured for Takeshi to get on the boat. "Sit, Takeshi," he said, his voice barely above a whisper. Takeshi, albeit perplexed, did as he was told. Gensho pushed the vessel off the shore and maneuvered it expertly to the center of the lake, letting the quiet lapping of water against the hull punctuate the serene quietness.

They sat there, the master and the merchant, in the heart of the still waters, surrounded by nothing but tranquil silence and the gentle embrace of the soft morning light. Neither spoke. As the boat floated peacefully, Takeshi experienced an inexplicable calmness. It was as if the stillness of the waters had an intoxicating power, gradually seeping into his distressed being. As the day unfolded, the sun ascending its celestial path, Takeshi found himself sinking deeper into the stillness. Time seemed to stand still, and within that suspended moment, he found his thoughts too beginning to halt their incessant rush. The outside chatter of his life ceased, and he was enveloped in a quiet, unseen before.

Suddenly, Master Gensho spoke, his voice a gentle ripple in the surrounding calm. "Takeshi, the boat and the lake, they coexist in harmony. The boat doesn't struggle to move against the tide or force its way through the waters. It simply allows the waters to hold it, to guide it. It is the art of letting be." Takeshi absorbed the words, feeling them echo within his being. He glanced at the lake, its surface a mirror of the sky, seamless and undisturbed. He felt a strange kinship with the boat, floating in harmony with the still waters, and a sudden clarity washed over him.

Master Gensho, noticing the change in Takeshi's countenance, smiled subtly. "Our worries, Takeshi, are like turbid waters. They murk our mind, obscuring the clear skies of joy and tranquility. But remember, Takeshi, like this boat, let your life float. Do not fight the currents of life but instead learn to navigate them. Allow the waters of existence to hold you, guide you, and you'll find serenity amidst the chaos."

Takeshi, taken by the profound simplicity of the monk's wisdom, felt a certain heaviness lift from his heart. As they rowed back to the shore, he realized he carried within him a newfound wisdom: the calm of letting be. He bid goodbye to Master Gensho, promising to return if he were ever to lose sight of his lessons. Under the watchful eyes of the Zen monk, Takeshi departed, feeling lighter, ready to embrace the currents of his life in a manner unlike before: with acceptance, serenity and a tranquil heart.

16

Wind Chimes' Music on a Breezy Day: Dancing with Change

Once upon a time, in a tranquil monastery nestled high in the lush green mountains, a Zen monk named Bankei lived in harmony with the world. Raised from childhood in these serene surroundings, Bankei had learned the delicate art of inner peace and adaptability. His wisdom was as vast as the endless skies, and his spirit was as light as the feathers of the swallows that dotted those vast, azure expanses.

One day, as Bankei was meditating beneath the sacred cherry blossom tree, he heard a faint tinkling sound. Opening his eyes, he looked towards the source. Hanging from the eaves of the monastery roof were delicate wind chimes, their bamboo tubes, seashells, and pieces of colored glass dancing in the breeze. Each gust of wind set off a melody so compelling that it seemed like an orchestra playing a symphony crafted by the cosmos itself. Bankei enjoyed this music. He would sit for hours, gazing at the chimes, each resonating sound echoing within him. He felt the music emanating from every fiber of his being, and with each note, he found himself flowing in synchronicity with the rhythm. The wind chimes, it seemed, were not just creating melodies but were also whispering the secrets of life to him.

During one breezy afternoon, while in this state of shared rhythm, Bankei noted something unusual. As a particularly strong gust of wind blew, one of the chimes turned turbulent, its melodious sound warping into a cacophonous note. It swung wildly, knocking against the others, and for a moment, the harmony was disrupted. Bankei's eyes were drawn to the chime. He observed its struggle against the wind, its resistance disrupting the serene melody. He stared at it thoughtfully, the dissonance echoing in his mind. Something within him stirred as he watched the chime battling the force of the wind.

However, this didn't disrupt his tranquillity. Instead, he continued to watch, his heart filled with compassion for the chime that was struggling, and he began to perceive the subtle teachings that the wind chime was offering. As the chime continued its frantic dance, Bankei rose from his meditative position and walked toward it. Gazing up, he noticed a small knot in the string that connected the chime to the roof. The knot had twisted and tightened, restricting the chime's movement and causing it to swing more violently with the wind. "Therein lays the cause," Bankei mused, his eyes reflecting deep understanding. He reached up, gently untied the knot, and allowed the chime to move freely again. As the wind blew, the chime once more swayed harmoniously, its music returning to the melodious tinkling that Bankei so enjoyed.

Returning to his spot under the cherry blossom tree, Bankei closed his eyes, a soft smile playing on his lips. The wind chimes continued their cosmic symphony, but now, each note resonated with a deeper meaning to him. The chime, he realized, had been trying to resist the natural flow of the wind - a struggle that only resulted in disharmony and distress. But once the resistance ceased, and it moved with the wind instead of against, the chime found its rhythm again. Bankei understood: just like the chime, when one resists the force of change, life loses its harmony. However, flowing with the changes, accepting them, dancing with them, restores the balance, the peace, and the rhythm.

Bankei's heart brimmed with gratitude for this newfound wisdom. He sent a silent thank you to the chime and the wind, his teachers for the day. The wind replied with a gentle gust, causing the wind chimes to tinkle in what seemed to Bankei like a chorus of shared joy and understanding. From that breezy day onward, Bankei carried this wisdom within him. No matter what changes life brought, he learned to dance with them, like a wind chime on a breezy day, and, in doing so, he found his life echoing with the sweet notes of serenity, adaptability, and joy.

17

Sun and Snowman:
Embracing Transformation's Warmth

Once upon a time in the quaint, peaceful village of Kinransho, a Zen monk named Tozan lived atop a secluded snowy mountain. Each winter, he would build a snowman outside his humble abode, a silent companion amidst the solitude.

One day, towards the end of the winter season, after a night of heavy snowfall, Tozan crafted a particularly beautiful snowman. He lovingly adorned it with a scarf woven from fallen leaves and a hat made of pine cones. He even gave it a pair of bamboo stick hands and two pebbles for eyes, completing the snowman with a warm, delightful smile. This snowman, unlike the ones he'd made before, seemed to possess a certain life-like quality that set it apart. Tozan cherished his creation and would spend hours each day, sitting beside it, in silence, observing the snowman with a smile. However, as the winter season began to wane, the sun climbed higher and higher into the sky each day, spreading its warm golden rays throughout the village. The snow on the mountain began to soften and drip, and Tozan watched as his beloved snowman began to shrink in size. The scarf of leaves sagged under the weight of the melting snow, and the pine cone hat slipped to the ground.

One might expect sadness or despair in Tozan's face as he watched his cherished companion diminish, but instead, there was a peaceful acceptance. He simply continued to sit beside the melting snowman, observing the transformation in silence. Down in the village, the children playing in the melting snow saw the sun as a destroyer, mourning the loss of their icy playgrounds. They saw the transformation as an end, a loss. But Tozan, the Zen monk sitting atop the snowy mountain, viewed the same sun and the same melting snowman, but with a different perspective. He saw a different kind of beauty in the transformation, a different kind of joy in the warmth.

While the snowman might have been melting away, Tozan's smile remained, as warm as the sun, as he watched the transformation unfold. Every morning, Tozan would replace the fallen pine cone hat and straighten the sagging leaf scarf, but each day, the snowman grew smaller. He saw how the pebble eyes that once sat high on the face of the snowman were now lower, the bamboo stick hands much closer to the ground. Yet, the snowman's smile never disappeared, for Tozan made sure to carve it afresh each day.

Even as the snowman dwindled, Tozan's own joy grew. He began to see the melting not as a loss but as a beautiful transformation. Like the snowman, he too was changing, constantly flowing with the rhythm of the universe. The children in the village could not comprehend Tozan's joy. They saw only the loss of the snow, the disappearance of their winter playmate. But Tozan embraced the warmth of the sun, the promise of spring, the return of chirping birds and blooming flowers. He saw life, not ending, but transforming, renewing.

One morning, Tozan emerged from his abode to find the snowman completely gone. The scarf of leaves lay on a patch of fresh green grass, the pine cone hat rested beside a budding flower, the pebble eyes and the bamboo stick hands had sunk into the soft earth. Tozan picked each item up, carefully dusting off the remnants of winter. He held them in his hands, feeling not a sense of loss, but a profound sense of serenity.

Tozan understood that while the snowman was gone, its essence remained. It had simply transformed, just as the seasons had. The snow had melted to water, nourishing the earth and helping the flowers to bloom. The snowman's joy was now in the blooming flowers, the green grass, the chirping birds. Like the snowman, Tozan realized, we too are ever-transforming, ever-evolving. As he sat there, under the sun's warm rays, with a smile as warm as his snowman's, Tozan felt an inexplicable joy. His heart was as light as a snowflake, his mind as clear as a sunny day. He had truly embraced the warmth of transformation.

18

Owl's Moonlit Queries:
Seeking Clarity in Shadows

In the tranquility of a small, secluded monastery, nestled amidst the verdant valleys and unrestrained wilderness, lived an old Zen monk named Hoshi. Hoshi was known far and wide for his wisdom and understanding of life's profound mysteries. Yet, even with his vast knowledge, he remained as curious as a child, forever in search of answers.

One soft, moonlit night, as the tranquility of the monastery was only interrupted by the distant hoot of an owl, Hoshi found himself unable to sleep. He stepped outside, drawn by the bewitching beauty of the moonlight dappling the monastery garden. As he walked, he contemplated the mysteries of the universe, his thoughts meandering like the swirling mists around him. In the stark contrast of the golden moonlight and inky shadows, he spotted an owl perched on a bent old tree. The creature's burnished eyes reflected the luminescent pool of moonlight, its gaze as deep and probing as the night itself. Hoshi, intrigued by the owl's solemnity, approached it.

"O wise owl," he greeted, "You are the sage of the night, the guardian of wisdom and the master of moonlit shadows. There is a question that troubles my mind. It is not new, and yet it is unanswered. Why is it that the shadows seem darker and more opaque when the moon is at its brightest?" The owl turned its head sideways, its luminous orbs met his, an air of mystique swirling around it. It remained silent, as if conveying that the answer lay not in words but in the wisdom of the moonlit night itself. Hoshi, however, was not disheartened. He knew that the question he posed was one that required insight rather than direct answers. Wisdom was a journey that he was willing to embark upon, even if it meant venturing into the unknown, shrouded depths of moonlit shadows. His pursuit of clarity, much like the owl's silent watch, was an endeavor that transcended the spoken word. In the tranquil silence of the night, with the owl as his only companion, Hoshi began another journey of introspection.

The moon continued its celestial journey across the star-studded canvas of the night, and Hoshi found solace in the company of the owl. He perceived the bird's silence not as a denial, but as an invitation to delve deeper into his own wisdom, to tread past the veneer of obvious answers and into the realm of profound understanding. As he meditated under the silver-washed glow of the moon, Hoshi closed his eyes and allowed his thoughts to meander freely. He began to understand that the question he asked was not about the shadows or the moonlight, but about the nature of life itself. Life was much like the dance of the moon and its shadows; it thrived in contrasts and thrummed with a rhythm born of harmony. Just as the brilliance of the moon seemed heightened by the deep shadows, one's joys gained significance because of the existence of sorrows, success because of failures, and wisdom because of ignorance.

The contrast of light and darkness wasn't a conflict, but rather a beautiful symbiosis that underlined the unity of existence. It was a gentle reminder that the world was an endless interplay of dichotomies, a poignant weave of the physical and the metaphysical, the seen and the unseen, the known and the unknown.

Opening his eyes, Hoshi turned to the owl. It had not moved, its gaze still firmly locked on the monk. But in its eyes, Hoshi saw a reflection of his newly found understanding. A soft hoot echoed in the quiet night, the owl's acknowledgment of his silent epiphany. Hoshi offered a small bow of gratitude to the wise bird and arose. As he returned to his chambers, he felt a deep sense of peace. No longer did the shadows of the night seem oppressive. Instead, they served as a testament to the radiance of the moon, a celebration of life's harmonious contrasts and a testament to the blossoming wisdom within his soul.

19

Cherry Blossom's Drift: Riding Life's Currents Gracefully

O nce upon a time, in the tranquility of a small monastery nestled deep within Japan's mountainous ranges, lived an old Zen monk named Bassui. He was revered for his wisdom, yet his ways were as gentle as the brush of a cherry blossom petal against the skin. Bassui often meditated under the ancient cherry blossom tree in the monastery courtyard, its blooms a vibrant pink during the spring.

One day, a young novice named Hiroto arrived at the monastery, seeking wisdom and peace. His life had been a tumultuous one, filled with obstacles and hardships. Hiroto hoped the monastery could provide him the sanctuary he needed to find meaning amidst the chaos. Bassui noticed the young man's struggle. Seeing the novice's restlessness, he decided to share an ancient Zen teaching that had guided him through life. But to convey the essence of the teaching, Bassui had a different plan in mind, one that would be more impactful than mere words.

Spring was on the horizon, and the cherry blossom tree was on the precipice of blooming. Bassui invited Hiroto to join him in cleaning the courtyard, hoping to prepare it for the upcoming bloom. Hiroto was confused but complied, assuming he was being taught humility through menial tasks. After days of sweeping and watering, the cherry blossom tree bloomed in full glory, showering the courtyard with delicate pink petals. The sight was breathtaking, and Hiroto stood in awe of the blossoms, floating and drifting in the wind.

Bassui smiled and said, "Now, Hiroto, your next task will be to catch the cherry blossoms as they fall from the tree. And remember, you must not allow them to touch the ground." Hiroto, although perplexed, nodded respectfully and prepared himself for the task that was seemingly impossible. As he positioned himself under the tree, he watched as the cherry blossoms began their elegant descent, each one moving to the rhythm of the wind. It was a dance of grace and chaos at once. He took a deep breath, ready to catch the falling blossom petals.

The task was far more challenging than Hiroto had anticipated, but he was undeterred, eager to understand the wisdom that Bassui promised. In the following days, Hiroto ran, jumped, and stretched, aiming to catch the falling petals. Yet each time, he found them just out of his reach, swaying away with the wind or falling too fast. His frustration grew, but he could not deny the calming effects of being amidst the cherry blossoms, their sweet scent filling his senses, their soft touch brushing against his skin.

One day, as he watched a particularly beautiful blossom twirl in the air, a sudden realization hit him. He understood that in his frantic efforts to catch the petals, he was disturbing the natural course of their fall. More importantly, he was missing out on the beauty of the moment – the flower petals dancing in the air, their serene journey to the ground, the joy they brought to the world by their mere existence. Hiroto fell into a peaceful silence, his frantic chase ceasing. He watched as the petals fell on their own, accepting their descent, and he found profound beauty in their journey, a symbolic representation of life's ups and downs. He realized that attempting to control the petals was like trying to control life's circumstances, an endeavor in futility.

Bassui, who had been observing Hiroto's journey, smiled. Hiroto looked at him, feeling a sense of serene understanding washing over him. Bassui asked, "What did you learn, Hiroto?" "I learned to cherish the journey, not control it," Hiroto answered. "Each petal, like life's moments, has its own path. Trying to control or alter it is futile and robs us of the joy of the present moment." Bassui nodded, his eyes filled with the wisdom of the ages. "Life, like these cherry blossoms, is a delicate dance between letting go and being present. Embrace it, Hiroto, and you will find peace amidst the chaos."

From that day, Hiroto lived with this newfound wisdom. He learned to ride life's currents gracefully, like the cherry blossom petals, finding peace, joy, and purpose in his life at the monastery.

20

Morning Moments with the Spiraled Fern: Starting Anew

In a secluded mountain temple lived an old Zen monk, Master Gichin. Every morning, as the first rays of the sun pierced through the morning mist, he would venture out into the temple garden. On one such morning, while the world was slowly waking, Master Gichin found a spiraled fern, just beginning to unfurl its leaves, nestled amongst the ancient stones. Intrigued by its delicate spirals, he sat down on the dew-kissed grass and regarded it with a serene smile. "Ah, a new beginning," he murmured to himself, his eyes sparkling with delight. For the next few days, Master Gichin started his mornings with the spiraled fern. He watched it unfurl, grow, and bloom under his attentive gaze. He marveled at the gradient of green that the spiraled fern exhibited, how it started as a soft pastel, unfurling into a deep emerald with time.

One morning, as he sat watching the fern, he was interrupted by a young monk, Hiroshi. The young monk, breathing heavily from his hurried ascent up the mountain path, bowed before Master Gichin, a troubled look on his face. "Master," he panted, "I am in turmoil. My mind is a storm of thoughts. I have lost my peace." Master Gichin regarded Hiroshi with a calm gaze. Turning his sight towards the spiraled fern, he motioned for Hiroshi to sit. He did not speak a word, but simply pointed at the fern.

Hiroshi, although puzzled, obeyed. He watched as the morning sun lit up the spiraled fern, casting a beautiful array of shadows on the stone beneath. The world around them began to awaken, the temple bells chimed, birds began to chirp, and the wind rustled through the leaves. Yet, in that moment, all that existed for Hiroshi and Master Gichin was the spiraled fern, basking in the morning sun. As they silently observed the fern, Master Gichin began, "Do you see, Hiroshi, how the fern unfurls its leaves? It was not long ago when it was nothing more than a tight spiral, holding within it great potential."

"Yes, Master," Hiroshi murmured, his eyes never leaving the plant. "You see," the old monk continued, "every sunrise is a reminder for the fern that it is time to grow. Some leaves unfurl faster, some slower, but each unfolds at its own pace, unhurried by the world around it." Hiroshi nodded, beginning to understand the lesson his master was imparting. Just as the fern, he too had the ability to take control of his own growth and the rhythm of his thoughts. "In life, just like the fern, our thoughts, feelings, and experiences unravel at their own pace," Gichin said, his voice barely above a whisper. "We must allow them to do so. When we resist or rush, when we dwell on the past or worry about the future, we lose our peace."

Gichin paused, letting the words sink into Hiroshi. Then he added, "Start anew, Hiroshi. With each sunrise, let your thoughts, your feelings, your experiences unfurl. Like the spiraled fern, be patient and embrace the process. It's the very essence of living." Hiroshi bowed his head, a sense of calm replacing the earlier turmoil. He realized every morning held the promise of a new beginning, a chance to unfurl his fears and worries, to grow and evolve, just like the spiraled fern.

From that day forward, Hiroshi began his mornings with the spiraled fern, a symbol of his newfound wisdom. And with every sunrise, he felt his inner storm quieting, replaced instead with a melodious tune of inner peace. The spiraled fern and its morning moments had taught him to see life differently, to live in the present, and to embrace the process of growth, starting anew every day.

21

Golden Fish's Grace Amidst Freeze: Staying Calm in Stasis

$\mathcal{I}$n the quaint village of Hanamachi, where the world barely stretched its fingers, a small, clear pond mirrored the whimsy of cherry blossom trees, the leaves scattering like fleeting dreams on its surface. Within the pond, a single golden fish darted amongst the pebbles, his scales shimmering like a sunbeam beneath the water.

Winter fell upon Hanamachi. It arrived quietly, like a contemplative monk, treading softly over the fallen leaves. The trees stood bare, their skeletal branches emblazoned against the solemn white sky. The once serene pond started to freeze, trapping the golden fish within its icy grasp. Yet, the fish remained unperturbed, his grace untouched by the encroaching frost.

In the village, the townsfolk were astir, anxious for the fish. How would it survive the bitter winter? Every morning, they huddled around the pond, their breath forming small clouds in the frigid air, watching for any signs of life beneath the sheet of ice. Each day, the golden silhouette of the fish could be seen, still darting between the frozen reeds and pebbles, as if the world around it remained untouched by winter's icy breath. Among the villagers, a young Zen monk named Saito watched the fish with a curious, yet calm eye. He was a silent observer, his presence barely noticed, like the whispering wind. Saito visited the pond every day, his footsteps leaving deep impressions in the snow. He knelt by the ice, watching the golden fish with a tranquil gaze, undisturbed by the biting cold or the hustle and bustle of the anxious villagers.

As days turned into weeks, the villagers' concern grew. The winter was harsher than they had ever known, and yet, the golden fish remained, undeterred by its icy prison. Saito, the Zen monk, continued his silent vigil, his calm equanimity matching the grace of the golden fish amidst the freeze. One day, as the sun was barely a pale smudge against the frosty sky, Saito finally broke his silence. He turned to the anxious villagers huddled in their winter garb and spoke, his voice as soft as falling snowflakes, "Why do you worry so for the golden fish? Look at him. He swims, he lives, undeterred by the cold. He has found peace in his present circumstance. Shouldn't we learn from him instead of fretting?" The villagers fell quiet, their worried eyes meeting the tranquil gaze of the monk. Saito continued, "Is the fish not like us? Yes, winter is harsh, but it is also a part of life. We can either resist it, growing anxious and fearful, or we can embrace it, finding beauty and peace within the frost."

Over the next few days, the villagers began to see the wisdom in Saito's words. They started observing the golden fish not with anxiety, but with a new sense of respect. As they watched the fish glide serenely amongst the frozen pebbles, they began to see the beauty in winter, the stark contrast of the golden fish against the icy blue, the serenity of the snow-covered village, the sharp, clean air. The fish, a symbol of grace and tranquility amidst adversity, became a reminder of the wisdom of acceptance and the strength of endurance.

And so it happened, that the harshest winter in Hanamachi became a time of profound personal growth and transformation for its villagers. The golden fish continued to swim, oblivious to the profound impact his existence had caused. As the cherry blossoms returned with the spring, Hanamachi was not just a village that survived a harsh winter, but one that thrived, blossoming into wisdom and tranquility, just like the golden fish amidst the freeze.

22

Conversations of Old Oak and Young Sprout: Learning Across Ages

*D*eep in the woodland sanctuary where the whispers of the wind danced with the rustling leaves, there stood an ancient oak. This grand old tree, with its gnarled branches reaching out like ancient arms and thick, rough bark worn like armor, was a witness to many a century and to the ever-changing world around it. Only a few yards away, nestled in the comforting shadow of the old oak, sprouted a young sapling. This sprout, flush with the vibrancy of its youth, was a tender green shoot, full of life, vivacity, and inquisitive wonder.

One fine dawn, as the first ray of sunlight lit the woodland, the young sprout swayed lightly and broke the silence. "Old Oak," it began, its voice as soft as the morning dew, "you've been standing majestically here for so long while I'm just beginning my journey. Can you share some of your wisdom with me?"

The ancient oak rumbled a chuckle, its voice as subtle and deep as the roots that anchored it to the earth. "Ah, sprout, your curiosity reminds me of my own youth, a time when I started as a mere acorn, full of dreams and questions. Your seeker's spirit is a testament to your potential," the old oak replied. "I do have so many questions, Old Oak," the sprout confessed, its voice quivering with anticipation. "The world seems so vast and I am just a tiny part of it." The old oak, sensing its youthful neighbor's uncertainty, shared a comforting thought, "In time, young one, you will learn to see the world differently. When I was young, I, too, felt small and insignificant.

But remember, the mightiest oaks start from small acorns. Though we start small, we are part of something much larger."

As the day unfolded, the woodland sanctuary resonated with the combined wisdom and curiosity of old and young, their shared laughter and profound silences, a testament to the timeless dance of wisdom across ages. The days passed as the warmth of the sun nurtured the young sprout, encouraging it to reach higher towards the sky. With each passing day, it grew taller, its tender green leaves soaking up the sunlight. All the while, the old oak stood tall and steadfast, a guardian of the woodland sanctuary, whispering tales of wisdom on the breeze.

One day, the young sprout, now growing steadily, asked the grand old oak, "What does it feel like to be so tall and mighty?" The old oak looked down at the sprout, its branches rustling as if in thoughtful contemplation. "Being tall gives me a broader perspective, little one. I can see far and wide. But remember, true might is not in towering over others but in the depth of our roots, the strength of our character." Taken aback, the young sprout pondered, "But how do you grow strong, Old Oak?" The old oak smiled, a rustle of leaves. "By weathering storms, young one, by embracing both rain and sunshine. By standing firmly in the face of adversity and not being afraid to endure hardships. That is how we grow strong."

Moved by the old oak's words, the young sprout silently pledged to face the world boldly, to weather life's storms, and most importantly, to grow – not just towards the sky, but deep down into the earth, forging a strong foundation. As the gentle moonlight bathed the woodland sanctuary, the young sprout fell into a peaceful slumber, buoyed by a newfound courage and resolve. The old oak, its branches cradling the moon, sent out whispers of wisdom on the cool night breeze, content in knowing another generation was ready to embrace the life lessons it had loved to share.

Waterfall's Roar, Pool's Calm: Balance After Turmoil

Once, in the heart of Japan's lush mountainous landscape, lived a Zen monk known as Master Kyoshi. He was a man of few words, yet his wisdom shone brighter than the morning sun. His home was a humble wooden monastery, nestled in the bosom of nature, next to a cascading waterfall. The waterfall was a spectacle of raw energy and unyielding power, its thunderous roar echoing through the valleys. Yet, at its foot rested a tranquil pool of water, still and calm, like the mind of an enlightened being. Master Kyoshi had a disciple, young and fervent with a heart full of questions. Taro was his name. One day, Taro approached Master Kyoshi as he was silently observing the waterfall. The roar of the falls was deafening, yet the monk, old and frail, seemed undisturbed, his gaze steady and his mind serene.

"Master," Taro began, raising his voice to be heard over the din of the waterfall. "The turbulence of the waterfall and the tranquility of the pool seem so mismatched, like fire and ice, night and day. Does this not defy the divine order of balance and harmony?" Master Kyoshi, his gaze still fixed on the waterfall, took a deep breath, letting the wild energy of the surroundings fill his being. His old, weathered hands were folded in his lap, a symbol of tranquility amidst the chaos.

"The waterfall and the pool are just like life, Taro," Master Kyoshi said, his voice rising softly above the roar of the waterfall. "There is a time for rest, and a time for motion. A time for silence, and a time for sound. Just like the waterfall and the pool, our lives too swing between the highs of turmoil and the depths of serenity." Taro respectfully bowed, his eyes glowing with the first flicker of understanding. However, the question that followed was even more pressing, revealing the depth of his curiosity and his thirst for wisdom.

"Master," Taro questioned, his gaze probing, "how do we find balance between these extremes? How do we avoid being consumed by the roar of the waterfall, and yet not become so placid that we are nothing but the still pool?" Master Kyoshi, breaking his gaze from the waterfall, turned to Taro. His eyes held a gentle firmness as he said, "Like climbing a mountain, Taro, balance is not reached at once, nor is it a static destination. It is a continuous journey, like the water's journey from the top of the waterfall to the tranquility of the pool. The waterfall's roar is not detrimental, but necessary. It is a release of energy, washing away the old, making way for the new, just like our struggles in life."

Master Kyoshi paused for a moment, letting his words sink into Taro's heart before continuing, "The tranquility of the pool is not stagnation, but a moment of rest and reflection, an opportunity to gather strength for the journey ahead, like our moments of peace and introspection. The balance comes not in suppressing one for the other, but in understanding and embracing both." Taro absorbed the words of Master Kyoshi, his eyes reflecting the wisdom shared. Looking back towards the waterfall and the tranquil pool, he found himself seeing them not as contradictions, but as necessary stages of a journey, each holding its unique value. That day, he learned that balance in life was not about eliminating turmoil or seeking constant tranquility, but about appreciating and learning from both. And in that wisdom, he found his first step towards inner peace and harmony.

24

Dragonfly, Mirage, and Desire's Trickery

Once upon a time in the quiet village of Yugen, there lived an old Zen monk named Kyo. He was known for his wise teachings and cheerful demeanor, often seen meditating beside the tranquil Onna Lake, where the lotus blossoms bloomed, painting the surface with hues of pink and white. One day, as he settled into his morning contemplation, a dragonfly darted past him. Its iridescent body shimmered under the morning sunlight, casting a tiny rainbow in its wake. The dragonfly, lost in its own world of flight and freedom, did not realize the mirage it was about to encounter.

Hovering above the lake surface, the insects' wings beat rhythmically, creating a melody that blended harmoniously with the tranquil nature's symphony. It dipped lower, drawn by the reflection of a magnificent lotus that appeared particularly vibrant on the water's surface. Unbeknownst to the dragonfly, the lotus it desired was merely a mirage created by the play of light and shadow on the water's surface. In its desire, the dragonfly plunged downwards, hoping to land on the beautiful flower, but found itself submerged in the cool water instead. Frantically, the tiny creature gathered all its strength and managed to escape the watery illusion, a little wiser and much wetter than before. From the corner of his eye, Kyo watched the dragonfly's struggle and eventual victory over the deceptive reflection. A gentle smile graced his lips, knowing that the dragonfly, in its innocence, had fallen for desire's trickery. But he also saw its resilience, its willingness to learn and adapt, a testament to the natural wisdom of all beings.

As Kyo continued his meditation, he became engrossed in the lesson the dragonfly had inadvertently imparted. He began to contemplate on desire's trickery and mirage, knowing that the teaching of this day was just beginning. Kyo sat in silence, meditating on the dragonfly's ordeal, his mind running with the rhythm of its wings against the water. He saw in its struggle, his own battle – the constant yearning for the material world, the illusions that were often mistaken for reality, and the deep plunge into disappointment when the truth revealed itself. It was desire's trickery at its finest. He remembered the times when he, too, had been drawn by the allure of illusion, just like the dragonfly. He had tasted the bitter fruit of disappointment and had risen, a little wiser but much humbler. He also thought about the times when he had conquered his desires and found himself greeted by the warmth of inner peace.

Kyo's gaze shifted from the tiny creature now drying its wings in the sunshine, back to the lake's surface, the water calm once again. He realized that just like the dragonfly, humans also often get distracted by the mirage of false desires but must learn to recognize and rise above them. He contemplated on the wisdom of the dragonfly and how it embraced life, without holding a grudge against the deceptive lotus. It did not indulge in resentment but instead chose to learn and keep moving. This, Kyo thought, is the true essence of life - to embrace the lessons that come our way, to rise above our failures, and to keep flying with grace, no matter how many times we fall.

The lesson was profound, and he decided to share this wisdom with his disciples. The dragonfly's resilience, its ability to distinguish the real from the illusion, and the way it moved on without dwelling in the past was a lesson for the villagers. He would teach them that the path to true joy and an ideal life wasn't chasing mirages but understanding, adapting, and embracing wisdom, just like the dragonfly.

25

Awakening of the Lotus:
New Beginnings Every Day

In the heart of the serene monastery nestled among the thriving bamboo forest, a wise old Zen monk named Master Kohaku peacefully lived. He was known far and wide for his profound wisdom and serene aura. With a gentle smile, he used to nurture the tender minds coming from far and wide, seeking solace and enlightenment. One day, a young novice, Kenji, arrived at the monastery. With a heart full of despair and eyes loaded with questions, Kenji was in search of a sanctuary to ease his troubled spirit. Greeted by the peaceful ambience of the monastery, Kenji was immediately in awe of its tranquility.

Master Kohaku, who was tending to the sacred lotus pond in the heart of the monastery, noticed Kenji. His eyes twinkled with a gentle compassion as he invited Kenji to join him by the pond. Kenji watched, captivated as Master Kohaku meticulously yet gently plucked a bud from the lotus pond and cupped it in his hands. The bud, closed tightly, was vibrant yet concealed within its layers.

"Do you see this lotus bud, Kenji?" Master Kohaku asked, his voice a gentle whisper echoing in the silence of the monastery. Kenji nodded, his eyes fixated on the tightly wound bud in the master's hands. "Yes, Master." "This bud holds a universe of beauty within its folds; an exquisite bloom waiting to emerge," murmured Master Kohaku, gazing at the bud. Kenji, puzzled, failed to grasp the depth of the master's words and asked, "But Master, how can it bloom? It appears to be very tight and confined."

Master Kohaku, with an understanding smile, responded: "You see Kenji, the bud is a living paradox. While it appears confined, it is, in reality, readying itself for a new beginning. Every morning, the sun gently caresses it, and the cool waters from the pond nourish it. Each day brings a new layer to unfurl, a little more of its inner beauty to reveal. It doesn't strive or stress to bloom; it simply allows nature's course to move through it."

"But the bud is not in haste, it is in patience. It knows that true blossoming comes not from a single dramatic change, but from a series of small, subtle shifts that accumulate over time," he continued, a serene smile playing on his lips. Kenji pondered over Master Kohaku's words, his furrowed brow reflecting his inner turmoil. "So, Master, you're saying that I...that we...are like this lotus bud?" Master Kohaku nodded, his eyes twinkling with wisdom. "Indeed, Kenji. Each of us carries an inner beauty, a potential to blossom. We may feel confined by our circumstances, trapped by our fears, but just like this lotus, we too are on the cusp of blooming. If we are patient and nurture ourselves with love and positivity, we'll find our petals unfolding in ways we never imagined."

Over the next few days, Kenji observed the bud in Master Kohaku's care. Slowly, it began to bloom, revealing an exquisite flower that radiated serenity and grace. And as the bud unfolded, so did Kenji. He began to understand that every new day was a chance for a new beginning, an opportunity to grow and blossom. Master Kohaku's words echoed in his heart, "Remember Kenji, no matter how tightly wound your bud of life seems to be, never lose faith in your ability to bloom. Just like this lotus, allow the gentle nurturing of time, patience, and self-love to guide you towards your own blossoming.

26

A Bee's Interruption:
Finding Joy in Unexpected Moments

*I*n a serene village at the foot of a verdant mountain, Master Zhu, the venerable Zen monk, lived a life of tranquility and contemplation. One bright, sunny afternoon, Master Zhu was in the midst of his daily meditation, his heart and mind synchronized with the peaceful rhythm of the universe. The fragrance of sweet grass wafted through the air, mingling with the scent of cherry blossoms that festooned the temple grounds. But amidst this tranquility, came a buzzing sound. A small bee, glowing gold in the afternoon sun, zipped and zapped around the monk's head. Disrupting the Zen-like quietness, it was seemingly intent on making its presence known. It fluttered around, hummed near his ear, and even landed on his calm, placid face. Yet, Master Zhu, with a gentleness that mirrored the breeze that rustled the cherry blossoms, neither swatted it away nor stirred from his position. He simply sat there, in the midst of his meditation, acknowledging the bee's existence but allowing it to be.

In the meantime, Li Wei, a young novice monk, watched this scenario unfold from a distance with a sense of agitation. He saw the bee as an annoying interruption to the Master's tranquil meditation. The constant buzzing and whizzing of the bee aggravated him, even though he was merely a spectator to this scene. Unable to withhold his discomfort, Li Wei rushed to Master Zhu's aid, a handcrafted fan in his grasp. He wildly waved it around, trying to shoo away the bee. Yet, Master Zhu, his eyes still shut, held up his hand stopping the young monk in his tracks. The buzzing continued, the bee continued its flight, and Master Zhu, with an enigmatic smile, resumed his meditation. The young monk, winded and frustrated, stepped back, failing to understand the Master's complacency amidst the persistent disturbance.

"Li Wei, why do you view the bee as an interruption?" Master Zhu asked, his voice as calm as the surface of a pond. He opened his eyes, revealing a depth of wisdom that belied his years. His gaze was steadfast on the young monk, encouraging him to think and question his perceptions. "The bee disrupts your meditation, Master," Li Wei responded, panting slightly from his exertion. "It buzzes around, distracting... interrupting your peace."

Master Zhu chuckled before responding. "Does the bee interrupt my peace, Li Wei? Or does your mind interrupt the bee's flight?" There was a twinkle in his eyes as he indulged in this little philosophical banter. Confused, Li Wei could only blink, unable to comprehend Master Zhu's words. The older monk continued, "The same sun that shines on us, shines on the bee. The same breeze that caresses our faces, carries the bee. The same universe that we inhabit, houses the bee. It is not an interruption, but a part of the universe's symphony. Just like us."

He paused, allowing the words to sink in before continuing. "Once we perceive everything around us not as interruptions or obstacles, but as part of the universe's eternal rhythm, life becomes a joyous dance, not a stressful battle." With his words hanging in the air, Master Zhu closed his eyes, entering his meditative state once again. The bee continued to buzz around, its flight a testament to the endless dance of life. Li Wei watched the insect, his irritation replaced with a newfound respect. His heart was lighter, his mind calmer.

As the sunlight danced on the cherry blossom leaves, he realized that wisdom could blossom even from a bee's buzzing. Master Zhu's words echoed in his mind, a lesson in finding joy in the most unexpected places. This moment, an interruption initially, had become a wellspring of wisdom, a moment of joy.

Pebble's Aspirations by the Sea: Dreams Beyond Size

*I*n a coastal village nestled between the mountain and the sea, lived a Zen monk named Hojo. Old yet spry, his crinkled eyes sparkled with wisdom. With a heart full of compassion, his mere presence offered solace to the villagers. One fine morning, as the sun painted the sky in hues of gold, Hojo took his usual stroll along the beach. His feet traced the line where the frothy waves met the sand, leaving behind a trail of footprints, only to be washed away by the next wave. It was during this peaceful walk that he noticed a tiny pebble lodged amidst the grains of sand. The pebble was an enchanting swirl of colors, an intricate pattern carved by time and the relentless sea. It was small, smaller than the other pebbles around, but it had a certain charm to it. Intrigued, Hojo picked it up and inspected it closely.

"Who are you, little one?" he asked, his voice carrying the warmth of the morning sun. "And what great dreams do you hold in your heart?" The pebble, though silent, seemed to resonate with a longing. It yearned to be more than just a trivial stone at the sea's edge. It had dreams beyond its size, dreams that towered over mountains and spanned across the endless blue sky.

"I am just a small pebble," it seemed to whisper, "with dreams larger than the sea. I wish to be a mighty boulder, standing tall against the wrath of the sea, shielding the shore from its fury. I want to be a beacon of stability amidst chaos, a symbol of strength and perseverance." Hojo listened to this silent plea, his wise eyes reflecting the pebble's audacious dreams. He held it in his palm, a small entity with aspirations that could dwarf even the mightiest mountain. The pebble was small, yet not insignificant, just like a single kind thought amidst a sea of negativity. The pebble was small, yet it dared to dream big.

The morning sun ascended higher in the sky, casting a warm glow on the pebble held gently in Hojo's hand, as the sea hummed a harmonious tune in the background, echoing the pebble's aspirations. Hojo held the ambitious pebble and gazed at it for a while, his mind painting a picture of the tiny stone's dream. The sea danced around his feet, pulling away the grains of sand, creating a metaphorical canvas for the Zen monk's thoughts. He visualized a small, insignificant pebble striving to become a stalwart boulder, standing immovable amidst the raging sea, a testament to unwavering strength. Raising his hand towards the sky, he said with a gentle smile, "Oh, audacious pebble, your dreams echo the teachings of life. Just as you, small as you are, yearn to be a mighty boulder, we, too, in our human lives, possess dreams that tower over us. We dream, we aspire, and we strive."

Hojo's gaze returned to the pebble in his hand. He saw that even in its smallness, it held a strength of purpose and a promise of potential. The pebble's dream was no different from the human experience, filled with hopes and aspirations that often seemed larger than life. With a chuckle, the old monk added, "Remember, little one, it's not the size of the dreamer, but the magnitude of the dream that truly matters. Someday, the forces of nature may grant your wish, turning you into a mighty boulder. But even before that happens, know that you already embody the strength and resolve of one."

Hojo gently placed the pebble back on the sand, the morning sun reflecting off its surface, making it shimmer in the golden glow. As he resumed his walk, he left behind the pebble that dared to dream big, a symbol of ambition and potential amidst the vastness of the sea. The pebble, though silent, seemed to understand the wisdom that Hojo shared. It gleamed under the sun, a tiny entity with dreams as vast as the sky, reminding anyone who looked its way that size doesn't define dreams or the ability to achieve them.

28

Children's Glee in Silent Snowfall: Joy in Simple Pleasures

*g*n the tranquil village of Shanti nestled at the base of Snowy mountains, resided a jovial monk named Tashi. One winter morning, as Tashi was meditating in his austere monastery, a flurry of laughter distracted him from his tranquil contemplation. Looking out the window, he saw the village children engaged in a friendly snowball fight. The pristine, undisturbed snow seemed to be in a playful dance, carried away by the winter wind. He observed the children's faces glowing in the frosty air, their laughter echoing in the chilly wind, the snow crunching underneath their boots. The sight was a harmony of pure innocence and vivacity; their joy infectious and refreshing. Tashi, too, felt an urge to join them, to partake in their wintry revelry. Yet he hesitated, believing that a monk should remain distant from such distractions.

Instead of joining them, he decided to watch the children from his window and enjoy the sight, absorbing the radiant joy reflected on their rosy-cheeked faces. The children, oblivious to the monk's observant eyes, continued to revel in the gentle snowfall, their laughter warming the frosty air. Every hushed flake that fell from the sky, every snowball thrown, every mischievous, gleaming eye added a new layer of fascination in the monk's curious gaze. The simple winter scene unfolding before his eyes was a play of color, laughter, and delight. The delicate beauty of falling snow, the vibrant joy of the children, and the rhythmic crunching of snow underfoot created a symphony of winter enchantment.

Tashi's heart filled with wonder at the scene. Among the children, there was no trace of sorrow, stress, or worry. They were living in the moment, relishing in the simple pleasure of snowfall. This spectacle, he realized, held a powerful lesson, one he could not have grasped through hours of meditation alone. Seized by a sudden inspiration, Tashi stepped away from the window, his robe rustling against the monastic silence. He took a moment to gather his thoughts and then moved towards the monastery door. As he stepped outside, the icy wind greeted him, cutting through his robe. It sharpened his senses, connecting him to the pure, untamed joy he had witnessed.

Tashi walked towards the laughing children, his footprints marking the untouched snow. A sense of anticipation filled the air as the children paused their game, watching the Zen monk approach. He bent down, cupped some snow in his hands and carefully crafted a snowball. His action was met with surprised gasps followed by giggles. The monk, revered for his wisdom and known for his serenity, was about to join them in their play. With a swift yet gentle motion, Tashi threw the snowball. It hit the giggling group of children, erupting an explosion of laughter. The children's delight was uncontainable as they included Tashi in their game, embracing his unexpected yet welcome participation. The air filled with the harmony of shared laughter, every sound amplified by the quiet snowfall.

The snowball fight was not just a game for Tashi. It was an unspoken lesson to the children about the joy in simple pleasures, the essence of living in the moment, the art of feeling alive. And for Tashi, it was an acquired wisdom, a realization that life's profoundest teachings could be found not just in silent contemplation but also in moments of laughter, in children's glee, in silent snowfall. As Tashi retreated to his monastery, leaving behind echoing laughter and joyous faces, he felt more enlightened. The day had offered him a new understanding of life and joy. Those children, unknowingly, had taught him that wisdom wasn't merely the product of introspection but also of shared moments of simple, unadulterated happiness.

29

Vase Awaiting Fragrance: The Potential Within

*I*n the humble village of Shodo nestled delicately between the verdant mountains and the tranquil river, there lived an old ceramist named Hiroshi. Hiroshi was known throughout the region for his remarkable skill of molding the coarse clay into beautiful pots and vases, each one a unique piece that mirrored his soul and wisdom. One day, as the sun painted hues of pink and gold across the sky, Hiroshi set about crafting a particularly exquisite vase. He molded the clay with ancient, gnarled fingers, a dance of artistry born from decades of dedication. Little by little, an object of beauty began to take shape. Its curves were perfect, its texture, flawless. It was a masterpiece, a testament to Hiroshi's lifelong dedication to his craft. Just as Hiroshi was applying the final strokes, a young boy from the village named Kenji approached the ceramist's hut. Kenji was often seen running errands for his mother, but today, curiosity had led him to Hiroshi's door.

The boy watched in awe as Hiroshi smoothed out the clay, his eyes reflecting the soft glow of the setting sun. The vase was empty, but it was beautiful, enchanting, almost magical. "It is so beautiful, Hiroshi-san," Kenji gasped, his eyes wide in wonder. "But why is it empty?" Hiroshi, who had been absorbed in his work, looked up at the question, his wizened eyes twinkling with an unspoken secret. He gazed at the young boy, then at the empty vase, a soft sigh escaping his lips.

"The vase is indeed empty, my dear boy," Hiroshi agreed, setting down his tools and cleaning his hands. "But I assure you, it is not without purpose." The edges of his mouth curled ever so slightly, a hint of a knowing smile that was like a promise of a story yet untold. As the last of the evening sun's rays disappeared into the night, Hiroshi beckoned Kenji closer. "Come, sit with me," Hiroshi said softly. "I will tell you a story about the potential within.

Kenji settled down beside Hiroshi, intrigued. The ceramist picked up the empty vase, his aged fingers tracing its smooth edges.

"In our lives, we all start as empty vessels, much like this vase," he began, his voice a melodious hum in the quiet evening. "But that doesn't mean we lack purpose or value. Each of us, like this vase, holds a unique potential within." Kenji looked at the vase again, his brows furrowed in thought. "The emptiness," Hiroshi continued, "is not a shortcoming but a chance. It's an invitation to be filled with experiences, knowledge, and wisdom, with love, kindness and joy." He then pointed out towards the cherry blossom tree nearby. "See those blossoms, Kenji? They were once tiny buds, empty of the beauty they now possess. But they held the potential for that beauty within them, much like this vase that awaits the fragrance of the flowers it's destined to hold."

Hiroshi placed the vase back on the table, his eyes meeting Kenji's. "You are also like this vase, Kenji. You might feel empty now, but you have immense potential within you. Your empty space is your power. It's your opportunity to learn, to grow, and to shape yourself. You are the artist of your life, and each day is a chance to mold your existence into a masterpiece." Kenji listened, his eyes wide with newfound understanding. The vase was no longer just a beautiful object to him. It was a symbol of potential, a reminder that his life was a canvas awaiting the strokes of his experiences. As the moonlight bathed the ceramist's hut, Kenji walked away, his mind filled with wisdom beyond his years. The vase might have been empty, but it was filled with a lesson he would carry forever.

30

Blind Monk's Colorful Visions: Seeing Beyond Sight

𝒢n the serene mountain village of Kinkan, there lived a revered Zen monk known as Master Yokota. He was not only respected for his profound wisdom and tranquil demeanor, but he was also admired for an unusual trait - Master Yokota was blind from birth. Yet, his lack of sight did not hinder him but instead, seemed to enhance his perception of the world beyond what the average eye could see. One day, his devoted pupil, Ito, asked him, "Master Yokota, how is it that you navigate the world without sight?"

Master Yokota merely smiled before he responded, "Ito, what do you see when you look at the world?" Taken aback by the question, Ito replied, "I see trees, mountains, rivers... people, Master." "Ah, but do you truly see?" Yokota asked, his face turning thoughtful. "Often, what we see with our eyes may be deceiving. We see the superficial, the exterior, the shell, but not what's underneath. We see a tree but fail to acknowledge the life it shelters, the air it purifies. We see a person, but seldom perceive their thoughts, feelings, their spirit."

As the week unfolded under Yokota's unerring guidance, Ito found himself questioning his perception of reality. He began to notice things he had previously overlooked: the chirping of the crickets in the evening, the rustling of the leaves by the wind, the faint tremors of the earth under his feet that signaled someone was approaching. One clear night, they sat under the infinite canvas of stars. Yokota asked, "Ito, what color is the sky tonight?" Ito glanced upwards, "It's black, Master, studded with white stars."

Master Yokota chuckled softly, "Every night, I see a different color. Sometimes it's the deep blue of tranquility, other times it's a warm and inviting gold. Tonight, I see an endless expanse of radiant silver. It's a beautiful world, Ito, if only we learn to truly see. Ito was silent, overwhelmed by the wisdom imparted by his blind master. As the days passed, he strived to embrace the world through his senses rather than mere sight. He listened to the people's unheard stories, felt the earth's untold tales, and started perceiving the world in a way he had never done before.

One day, during their morning meditation, Master Yokota broke the silence, "Ito, how do you perceive this moment?" Ito closed his eyes, breathed deeply, listened to the distant chirping of birds, felt the soothing breeze on his skin, and tasted the sweet air laced with the scent of cherry blossoms. "Master, I see it as an orchestra of tranquil harmony," he replied, his voice barely above a whisper. Yokota smiled, his face reflecting a sense of serene satisfaction. "Yes, Ito. You're learning to truly see, to understand the world beyond its facade. It's not about colors, shapes, or light. It's about understanding the world with your heart and your spirit."

Ito spent the following years under Yokota's tutelage, learning to see beyond sight. He began to perceive the world's vibrant colors through his heightened senses and deep understanding. The world seemed to bloom around him, rich with new experiences, sounds, scents, and emotions that he had previously been oblivious to. With this newfound perspective, he found himself free from negativity. He discovered joy in the simplest things and embraced a life filled with wisdom and tranquility. Ito had learned a profound lesson - to truly see, one has to look beyond sight, to perceive with the heart, and to understand with the spirit. It was a lesson he would cherish, a gift from the blind monk who saw the world in the most colorful way.

31

Night Whispers of Rustling Leaves: Nature's Comforting Lullaby

In the heart of a bustling city that never slept, resided a time-worn monastery, a sanctuary of tranquility amidst the chaos. It was home to an elderly Zen monk, Master Hakuin, who lived a life of simplicity and wisdom. One sultry summer night, unable to find solace in sleep, Hakuin found himself sauntering through the monastery's lush courtyard. The night was darker than the deepest ink wash, making the monastery's pagoda spires barely visible. Yet, the silver crescent moon hung in the sky, casting an ethereal glow that bathed the world in a soothing hue. As he strolled, Hakuin's bare feet brushed against the dew-kissed grass, leaving a trail of wet footprints behind. The crickets began their nightly symphony, breaking the silence. In the monastery's heart stood a magnificent cherry blossom tree, ancient and wise, its drooping branches adorned with delicate, pale-pink blossoms. The leaves rustled invitingly, whispering a lullaby crafted by nature itself to lull the world to sleep.

Hakuin settled under the cherry blossom tree, his aged eyes reflecting the glimmer of the moon. He watched as a solitary petal detached itself from its blossom and spiraled gently downwards, performing a silent ballet before finally blending with the other fallen petals on the ground. The whispers of the leaves grew louder, a calming rhythm that echoed through the courtyard. They were the voices of nature, soothing, yet persistent, often unnoticed in the cacophony of city life, but here, in the hush of the night, they were comforting and serene.

The world around him was asleep, yet the rustling leaves and the moon's soft glow seemed more alive than ever. It was a contrast, a beautiful harmony of rest and activity, silence and whispers, darkness and light. As the whispers of rustling leaves continued their comforting symphony, Hakuin found himself lost in a newfound sense of peace, a gentle reminder that even in the heart of the night, there was life and beauty to be found. Sitting under the sheltering branches of the cherry blossom tree, Hakuin closed his eyes, letting the whispers of the rustling leaves wash over him, their rhythmic sway a soothing balm to his restless spirit. The moonlight seeped through the dainty petals, casting an intricate dance of light and shadow on his weathered face. A sense of tranquility filled his being, like a stone that sinks effortlessly into the deep recesses of a calm pond.

Opening his eyes, Hakuin looked up and saw the moon—poised like a pearl against the black fabric of the night, a beautiful solitary beacon. The moon's glow transformed the ordinary into the extraordinary; it made the dew drops on the leaves glisten like precious diamonds and the cherry blossoms glowed with an almost supernatural radiance. It was a monochrome world under its radiance, yet filled with a profound richness that spoke to the soul. As Hakuin sat there, a gentle breeze picked up, making the cherry blossom tree sway. The petals, caught in the wind's playful grasp, started a swirling dance in the air before carpeting the ground. The rustling of leaves intensified as if echoing his heartbeat, their whispers more pronounced. It was a symphony of life amidst profound silence—a testament to the resilience of nature.

The whispers of the rustling leaves and the moon's tender glow served as a reminder to Hakuin—and to anyone who cared to listen—that peace and beauty could be found amidst the chaos, in the ordinary, and even in the heart of the night. Nature was there, with its reassuring rhythm, whispering the simple truth: life is a balance of activity and rest, light and darkness, sound and silence.

Serenity, he realized, wasn't about running away from the noise but finding peace within it. With a content sigh, Hakuin finally embraced sleep, cradled by the night whispers of rustling leaves, the comforting lullaby of nature, under the watchful glow of the moon.

32

Bamboo Standing Tall in Winter: Resilience in Adversity

$\mathcal{I}$n the small, peaceful village of Kurokawa, nestled amidst the sprawling hills and tranquil rivers, lived an old Zen monk named Haruki. He was revered and respected by the villagers for his profound wisdom and serene demeanor. Haruki lived in a small, humble hut on the outskirts of the village, beside a dense bamboo grove that whispered secrets to the wind. One clear, cold winter day, a young farmer named Katsu visited Haruki. He was desolate, his spirit crushed by a series of unfortunate events. His rice fields had been devoured by pests, his house had been ravaged by a sudden fire, and his wife had fallen gravely ill. The once robust and cheerful Katsu now walked with a hunched back and sorrowful eyes which reflected his tale of adversity.

As Haruki listened to Katsu's troubles, his eyes grew soft, filled with empathy. He invited Katsu into his small hut, offering a warm cup of green tea and a chance to seek refuge from the piercing winter wind. The rustic home, modestly adorned with simple daily objects, had a peaceful air around it, soothing Katsu's restless soul, even if just a little. After a few moments of silence, Haruki softly suggested, "Katsu-san, join me for a walk."

Despite the biting cold, Haruki led Katsu down the frost-covered path to the bamboo grove. The tall bamboo stalks stood resilient against the cold, their leaves rustling gently as if whispering to each other. The sight was majestic, their towering height a stark contrast to the surrounding snow-covered landscape. Katsu, awestruck by the unusual sight, whispered, "How do they survive the harsh winter?"

Haruki simply smiled, his eyes twinkling with a wisdom borne of years, and said, "The way of the bamboo is to bend but not break. It's their secret to weathering the storm."

For a moment, Katsu stared, unsure of what Haruki was trying to say. As the cold wind blew, rustling the bamboo leaves into a chorus of whispers, Katsu began to ponder the old monk's cryptic words. Haruki gestured towards the bamboo grove as he continued, "You see, Katsu-san, the bamboo does not resist the cold. It does not stiffen against the wind, but rather, sways with it. It doesn't fight what it cannot change, but adapts to it. It remains firmly rooted in the ground, yet flexible enough to dance with the wind. Even during the harshest winter, the bamboo stands tall, in stoic resilience. It is not the cold that the bamboo fears, rather, it embraces it, standing tall, unyielding, and strong." Katsu, still perplexed, watched how the bamboo stalks gracefully danced in the wind. He had never viewed his adversity from this perspective before.

Haruki's serene voice echoed, "Much like the bamboo, Katsu-san, we too have to learn to lean into our struggles and not resist them. We need to remain rooted in our strength, yet flexible enough to adapt to the change. Our adversities are the cold winters of our life. If we learn from the bamboo, we too can stand tall in the face of adversity, just as the bamboo stands tall in winter." Spellbound by Haruki's profound wisdom, Katsu felt his shrunken spirit stir awake. He stared at the bamboo stalks in awe, their resilience resonating with his beaten spirit. A slow, steady stream of understanding filled him, illuminating the path he needed to take.

As they walked back, Katsu's shoulders were not as hunched and his eyes not as heavy. The farmer, who had come seeking solace, left with a newfound understanding of resilience in adversity. He knew his path was not easy, but the sight of bamboo standing tall in winter was etched deep within his heart. And with the wisdom of the old monk to guide him, he was ready to face his winter, just like the resilient bamboo.

33

Phoenix's Rise:
Renewal from Life's Ashes

Once upon a time, in a remote village nestled amidst the mighty Himalayas, there lived an old Zen monk named Ryushin. Ryushin lived in an ancient temple that was perched precariously on the edge of a stormy cliff, but this did not trouble him. He welcomed the isolation and the constant reminder of life's fragility. One day, a traveler named Akio came to the village. Akio was a tall, lanky man, with a sun-beaten visage that spoke volumes of his many years wandering the globe. He was known for his boisterous laughter and merry stories he shared with anyone who would lend an ear. Yet, beneath the jovial facade, Akio was a man profoundly scarred by life's many trials. He carried the burden of his past like an albatross around his neck, unable to let go, unable to move forward.

Akio sought the wisdom of Ryushin, hoping to find solace and perhaps a solution to his internal turmoil. He trekked the treacherous trail leading to Ryushin's sanctuary and arrived just as the sun was setting, painting the sky with hues of brilliant orange and deep blue. Ryushin, sitting in his simple robe, was as still as the mountains that surrounded him. His eyes were closed, utterly absorbed in meditation. However, the moment Akio's footsteps echoed in the ancient temple, Ryushin opened his eyes. He looked at Akio. Not just at his sunbeaten face and tired eyes, but at the despair he carried with him.

"Welcome, traveler," Ryushin greeted Akio, his voice calm as a summer's breeze, "You have come a long way." Akio nodded, sinking down onto the floor across from Ryushin. He was silent for a moment before he hesitantly began to speak. He shared his story, his burdens, his regrets, and his hopes, his voice echoing in the vast emptiness of the temple. Ryushin listened attentively, nodding occasionally in understanding. Once Akio finished, the silence lingered for a moment before Ryushin finally broke it.

"Life," Ryushin began softly, "is much like the phoenix." His eyes twinkled, reflecting the dying embers of the sunset. "It burns, it suffers, it dies... only to rise again from its ashes." Akio's brow furrowed, confusion knitting his features. The monk's cryptic metaphors were not giving him the solace he sought. Sensing Akio's struggle, Ryushin decided to elaborate.

"My dear Akio," he started, "your past, your regrets, your burdens - they are like the fire that burns the phoenix. It hurts, yes. But remember, the phoenix does not defy the fire. It embraces it. It accepts the flames, for it knows that rebirth awaits on the other side. Only through this acceptance can it rise once more, stronger and more beautiful than before." Akio was silent, his eyes glistening with the revelation, staring at the monk.

"Phoenix's rise," Ryushin continued, "does not deny its history of flames. Instead, it symbolizes rebirth, renewal. Your past, Akio, is not a chain that restrains you. It is a fire from which you can rise, renewed and transformed. Hold your past like the phoenix holds its flames. Allow it to burn, to hurt, to end. Then, from its ashes, rise like the phoenix, mightier than ever before."

As the last rays of the sun disappeared, Ryushin rose to his feet, leaving Akio with his thoughts. He didn't need to look back to know that he had ignited a spark of wisdom in the traveler's heart. With time, that spark would grow, allowing Akio to face his past, embrace it, and ultimately rise from it, just like the phoenix from its ashes. The story of the Phoenix's Rise was not just a tale. It was a path towards renewal; a guide to conquer negativity, and most importantly, a beacon of hope for those lost in the wilderness of their past.

34

Harmony of Cat's Purr and the Bell's Ring: Inner and Outer Peace

The soft morning light barely peeked through the cherry blossom trees when the distinct sound of a temple bell echoed in the air. The Zen monk, Takumi, stepped out of his small, austere room into the vibrant garden. The grass, still damp with dew, felt cold against his bare feet. He took a deep breath, savoring the scent of blossoms that filled his lungs, their sweetness a reminder of the fleeting beauty of life. The old Zen temple, nestled high in the mountains, was home to all sorts of creatures, cohabiting in harmony. Among them was a scruffy tabby cat, Miyako, who had made her home here one cold winter's day and never left. As Takumi stepped onto the stone path, Miyako appeared, her feline grace undeniable despite her unkempt coat.

Miyaki wound her way around Takumi's legs, purring softly. The purr was a low, comforting rumble that seemed to resonate directly with his heartbeat, as though the cat and the monk were tuning into the same cosmic rhythm. Takumi gently stroked Miyako's back, the purr growing louder, a humble chant for peace and tranquility. Just then, the bell tolled once more. Its deep, resonant sound filled the air, vibrating through the very stones of the temple. The bell's ring mirrored the solemn mountain peaks, the peaceful rustle of the leaves, and the steady hum of the world itself. It was a testament to the harmony that existed between the inner world and the outer, a melodic reminder of the musical intertwining of the spirit and the material.

The purr and the bell rang in unison, creating a symphony that soothed Takumi's soul. He closed his eyes and let the duet wash over him, a beautiful interplay of inner peace and outward harmony. His heart danced to the rhythm, his spirit felt as light as the blossoms that swirled in the early morning breeze. As he stood there, bathed in the warmth of the rising sun, the monk couldn't help but feel the profound interconnectedness of all things, the remarkable symphony of life unfolding in perfect harmony. As the rhythmic symphony played on, Takumi slowly knelt down, his old joints protesting slightly, and extended his hand to Miyako. The small cat leaned into his pat, her purrs reverberating across his skin like the softest of whispers. He tenderly cradled her, his wrinkled hands comfortable and familiar against her matted fur. Unfazed by the abrupt elevation, she simply closed her eyes and continued her comforting song.

The bell's deep echo lingered in the air, harmonizing with the delicate purr. It was as if the bell was ringing for Miyako, and she was purring for the bell. An extraordinary dance of peace, a unique waltz that only they understood. Their distinct sounds melding together to create a beautiful melody that not only soothed the listener but also cleansed the spirit. As the sun began to climb higher into the sky, the harmony between the bell and the cat's purr grew richer, fuller. It resonated deep within Takumi, filling him with a profound serenity that washed away any remnants of stress or negativity. His heart pulsed in rhythm with the sounds that encapsulated him, each beat a testament to his intrinsic connection with the world around him.

Embracing Miyako, he looked up and noticed how the sun's ray was refracted by the dew on the cherry blossoms, casting a kaleidoscope of colours across the garden. This spectacle of nature's grace, coupled with the divine harmony between the bell and the cat's purr, filled him with joy - a simple, pure joy that came from appreciating the beauty of existence. Takumi's spirit felt invigorated. As the last echo of the temple bell faded and Miyako's purr softened into silence, he realized that this moment was a reflection of life's harmonious orchestra. It was a reminder to appreciate the symphony of existence, to permeate his inner and outer world with peace, and to embrace the wisdom that life, in all its exquisiteness, is a beautiful cycle of interconnected melodies.

35

Moon's Quest over a Restive Pond: Searching for Serenity

*I*n a secluded mountainous region of Japan, there resided an old Zen monk named Ryo. His small abode was placed at the foot of a towering mountain, adjacent to a restive pond, known as the 'Koi Pond of Eternal Reflection'. Its surface was a ruffled canvas of dreams, fed by the mountain spring and distracted by the playful Koi, the revered fish of the land. The pond was his solace, a mirror reflecting the moon's journey across the night sky, and the monk's journey within his own soul. One evening, under the gentle glow of a waxing moon, Ryo sat by the pond, engrossed in deep meditation.

The moon's soft light delicately skimmed across the restless water, setting aglow the vibrant scales of the koi. The night was filled with a symphony of nature: the whispering wind, rustling leaves, and the intermittent splash of playful Koi disrupting the otherwise serene water. But Ryo's mind was far from still. He was troubled, caught in the relentless waves of worldly worries. His usual calm demeanor was replaced by a brewing storm of unrest. Tonight, the moon, his silent companion, seemed distant, veiled behind a curtain of clouds, mirroring his own obscured peace.

Ryo broke his meditation, his eyes drawn to the moon's reflection dancing on the restless water. He admired how the moon's undeterred quest manages to find tranquillity amidst the pond's chaos. Yet, he wondered why his own quest for inner peace was fraught with so many perturbations. Intrigued, he decided to spend the rest of the moonlit night by the pond, hoping to understand its secret. Little did he know, this quest of understanding the moon's journey over the turbulent pond would take him on a path of profound wisdom and serenity.

His heart stirred with anticipation, while the wind carried his silent prayer, "Moon, reveal to me your quest, show me the path to tranquility in unrest." The moon glanced back at him through the clouds, as if knowing that a beautiful journey was about to unfold. As Ryo sat in silent communion with the moon, the midnight wind rustled the cherry blossom trees, showering him with a cascade of petals. Each petal that kissed the restive pond sent ripples across the moon's reflection, creating an array of serene chaos. The moon's image, though distorted, was still visible, its calm light a stark contrast to the agitated water.

A realization dawned upon Ryo. His mind, too, was like the pond, disturbed by the petals of worry, fear, and doubt. Yet, amidst the turbulence, the moon's reflection - his inner peace - remained present, albeit distorted. His quest was not to seek tranquility in a sea of serenity but to find it amidst the roar of chaos. With renewed understanding, Ryo returned to his meditation, embracing the ripples of thoughts instead of pushing them away. He observed each one without judgment or resistance, allowing them to come and go, just like the petals on the pond. He found solace not in the absence of these thoughts, but in the acceptance of their existence. The moon's reflection on the pond started to become more pronounced, no longer veiled by the curtain of clouds. Unfazed by the restive koi or fluttering petals, it shone with a serene glow, bearing witness to the silent dance of life beneath it. Ryo, too, found his inner peace illuminating brighter, undeterred by the ripples of his thoughts.

As dawn approached, Ryo opened his eyes, a soft smile playing on his lips. He thanked the moon, whose silent quest over a restless pond taught him to find tranquility amidst unrest. The quest had indeed opened a path to profound wisdom and serenity, and Ryo couldn't help but feel a deep sense of gratitude for the journey he had embarked upon. The wind carried his silent prayer once more, "Moon, thank you for your guidance. I now understand, tranquility is not the absence of unrest, but the presence of peace within it." The moon, now setting, seemed to smile back, leaving behind the first rays of dawn as a beautiful testament to Ryo's blossoming wisdom.

36

Feather's Journey on Guiding Breezes: Trusting Unseen Forces

O nce upon a time, in a humble monastery perched high on a hill, a novice monk named Daishin lived with his wise master, Kainan. The monastery was surrounded by a vibrant forest of whistling pines, cherry blossoms, and ancient oaks. The landscape was often painted with the playful activities of birds, their feathers dancing in the wind like soft, ethereal dreams. One day, while sweeping the cobblestone paths of the monastery, Daishin found a solitary feather lying still amidst the leaves. It was a magnificent feather, its iridescent colors shimmering in the sunlight, painting a symphony of hues on the old, worn stones. Daishin held it up against the sky, admiring it. But as he did, a gust of wind swept the feather from his hand. He watched as it danced in the wind, twirling this way and that, before it disappeared into the vast blue yonder. Throughout the day, Daishin couldn't help but contemplate the feather, its journey, and the unseen forces that guided it. Troubled by these swirling thoughts, he sought the wisdom of his master, Kainan.

Daishin knocked gently on the door of the master's chamber, hearing the soft echo fill the room before the sound was swallowed by the silence. As he entered, he saw Kainan seated on the floor, a peaceful smile playing on his lips as he contemplated a single cherry blossom in a delicate porcelain vase. "Master," Daishin began, his voice barely a whisper. "Today, I found a feather of extraordinary beauty. As I held it up to admire it, a gust of wind swept it from my grasp. The feather danced on the wind, trusting the unseen force to guide it.

Its journey seemed uncertain, yet it went willingly. I find myself pondering on this, but the answers elude me."

Kainan remained silent for a moment, his gaze never leaving the cherry blossom. Then, he simply said, "Perhaps the feather has something to teach us, Daishin." He paused before continuing, "Let us reflect on this a while longer." Daishin nodded, thanking his master before retiring to his quarters. There, amidst the silence punctuated by the occasional rustle of leaves outside, Daishin pondered over his master's words. He found himself entranced by the imagery of the feather, its dance, and the unseen breezes guiding it.

Days turned into weeks as Daishin continued his contemplation. He went about his daily duties in the monastery, but the image of the feather was never far from his thoughts. One day, while meditating in the garden, he found his answers. With his eyes closed, Daishin could feel the warmth of the sun on his skin, the caress of the wind in his hair, and the rustling of leaves. He realized that like the feather, he too was on a journey. He was guided by unseen forces - the teachings of his master, the sacred scriptures, his own intuition - just like the feather was guided by the wind.

Just as the feather trusted the wind to carry it, Daishin realized he too had to trust these unseen forces guiding him. The journey may seem uncertain, and he may not know where he was headed, but he needed to embrace the unknown. Like the feather, he found beauty not in the destination but in the journey itself, in the dance of life. A wave of tranquility washed over Daishin as this realization dawned on him. He finally understood the wisdom his master had wanted him to discover. With newfound clarity and a heart filled with joy, Daishin walked back to the master's chamber.

"Master," Daishin said, his voice reflecting his inner peace, "I now understand. Like the feather, I too must trust the unseen forces guiding me. The beauty lies not in the destination but in the journey itself." Kainan simply smiled, his eyes reflecting the pride he felt for his pupil.

37

Deer's Brave Stand: Courage Amidst Challenges

*I*n a quiet corner of the ancient forest, there lived a timid, young deer named Davu. He was slender and swift, with sparkling eyes filled with innocence. Yet behind his evanescent charm was an underlying layer of anxiety. The forest was full of danger, and because of his timidity, Davu had never ventured far from his safe haven, the lush meadow, where his mother had told him stories of the cruel and unforgiving world. One day, a terrible wildfire ignited, spreading uncontrollably through the forest. Alarmed by the approaching danger, the animals began to flee. However, Davu found himself frozen in place, overpowered by an unshakeable fear. The entire forest seemed shrouded in a monstrous, fiery beast, its flames licking hungrily at the trees.

Suddenly, the legendary Zen Monk appeared before Davu amidst the chaos. He was a sturdy, elderly man with wisdom radiating from his serene eyes. His presence felt like the calm eye of a storm. "Davu," he said, his voice echoing through the smoke-filled forest, "the real enemy is not the fire or the world outside. It is the fear in your heart." Davu looked at the Monk, his eyes filled with confusion. The Zen Monk continued with an unwavering calmness, "Courage is not the absence of fear, but the willingness to face it."

As the fire was closing in, the Zen Monk pointed towards a narrow, winding path leading out to safety. "Beyond that path," he stated, "lays an oasis where the fire cannot reach. You must lead the animals there, Davu."

Davu looked at the path, then at the terrified animals, and finally at the Zen Monk. He was faced with a choice - to cower in fear or stand tall amidst the challenges. The decision he was about to make would not only shape his destiny but also the fate of the entire forest community. Davu's heart pounded as he absorbed the monk's words. Fear, he realized, had been his constant shadow, limiting him to the confines of his known world while the vast unknown beckoned. His entire existence had been shaped by fear - fear of the unknown, fear of the outlying dangers, fear of stepping out of his comfort zone. And now, it had the power to cost him his life, and the lives of his fellow creatures.

A sudden wave of understanding washed over him. The Zen Monk was right - fear was not an external entity, but an internal monster that he needed to conquer. It was his journey, his fight. And it began with acceptance, with the recognition that fear was a part of him, but it did not define him. With newfound resolve, he turned to the path ahead. It was unknown, winding, fraught with unseen perils. But it was also their only way to escape the fiery inferno.

His slender legs trembled, but he forced himself to move. With each step he took, he felt his fear dissolving, replaced by a strange, exhilarating sense of empowerment. He was not running from fear anymore; he was racing against time to save his home, his companions. His swift movements sent a message to the other animals. One by one, they began to follow him, their faith placed on Davu's slender shoulders. The young deer, once timid and fearful, was now leading the entire forest towards salvation.

The Zen Monk watched from the distance, a smile of approval etched on his wise face, as the young deer emerged from the shackles of his fear and embraced the power of courage. Davu had not only accepted the Monk's wisdom, but he had also blossomed it into an act of bravery, an act that had potentially saved them all from the wrath of the wildfire. And so, in the face of adversity, the timid deer became the forest's brave guide, proving that courage indeed stands tall amidst challenges, forever outlasting fear.

38

Lantern's Glow on Shadowed Paths: Hope Illuminating Doubt

Once upon a time, in the quiet tranquility of the Zen monastery, lived an aged monk named Keizani. Keizani, a man of profound patience, had a profound propensity for silence and solitude. His days were filled with echoing chants, long meditations and meticulously tending to the monastery's verdant tea gardens. One chilly autumn night, Keizani was making his customary walk around the monastery grounds, carrying a small lantern for company. The wind was howling through the skeletal boughs of the trees, creating a symphony of rustles and whispers. The flickering light of the lantern cast eerie shadows on the cracked stone pathway, making his surroundings look like an intricate dance of light and darkness.

As he ambled down the serpentine path, the glow from the lantern fell on an ancient Bodhi tree at the edge of the gardens. Keizani was instantly drawn to it. He had heard tales of the tree from his master. They spoke of its ageless resilience, wisdom, and the secrets it held in its gnarled branches. Yet, the shadows cast by the tree were dense and foreboding, seemingly insurmountable. Despite the comforting glow of his lantern, Keizani felt a shiver of trepidation grip him. For a moment, Keizani considered retreating, letting the uncertainty scare him away from the looming shadow of the tree. But he remembered the teachings of his master, who often said, "Fear and doubt are but shadows. They can't survive in the presence of the shining light of wisdom."

So, with a deep breath, he decided to walk toward the Bodhi tree, lantern held high. As he approached the tree, the long shadows started to recede, giving way to the gentle, warm light. Keizani continued his journey, the glow of the lantern illuminating his path, and the shadows dancing rhythmically around him. As Keizani drew closer to the Bodhi tree, he slowly began to see the grandeur of the ancient entity. The intricate patterns etched onto the bark whispered stories of centuries of relentless endurance and unwavering resilience. As the vibrant glow of the lantern washed over the Bodhi, he felt a strange sense of calm and serenity envelop him. The shadows that once seemed daunting now seemed faint, their might diminishing under the radiance of the lantern.

Slowly, Keizani lowered himself onto the dew-kissed grass beneath the Bodhi, placing the lantern at the base of the tree. As he sat there, bathed in the soft, reassuring glow of the lantern, he found his fear and doubt ebbed away, replaced by an overwhelming sense of hope and comfort. He began to meditate, his mind opening to the wisdom and the teachings of the Bodhi. The wind rustled through the leaves, whispering ancient teachings, stories of ages gone by. The gentle sway of the branches in rhythm with his breath, the rustling of the leaves in tune with his heartbeat, brought forth a profound sense of connectivity and peace.

Hours slipped by as Keizani lost himself in the tranquility of the moment. When he finally opened his eyes, the first rays of the sun were painting the sky in hues of gold and crimson. The lantern's glow had faded, giving way to the break of dawn. Yet, the once foreboding shadows were nowhere to be found. As he stood up to continue his journey, Keizani felt lighter. His heart was filled with newfound wisdom, his spirit buoyed by hope. The Bodhi tree, with its shadowy threats, had turned into a source of enlightenment, all thanks to the glow of the lantern, a symbol of wisdom and faith that illuminated the path of understanding and resilience.

For Keizani, it was another day, another lesson learned. A lesson that assured him that no shadow was too dark or daunting when faced with the glow of hope and wisdom. And it was this thought that comforted him as he walked away, leaving the Bodhi tree basking in the early morning sun.

39

Ripples from a Simple Stone: The Power of Presence

*I*n a small village, in the rolling hills of the countryside, a single Zen Monk resided. Known for his profound wisdom and tranquility, he emanated an aura of calm that even the most chaotic minds found soothing. One warm afternoon, while the sun generously showered its light on the clear brook nearby, the Monk was found sitting on a moss-coated rock by the water, his serene gaze fixed on its steady, tranquil flow. A young boy from the village, Yuki, happened to pass by. Noticing the Monk, the boy's curiosity was piqued. He had often heard tales of the Monk's wisdom and desired to acquire some of it for himself.

Yuki approached the Monk and respectfully bowed, "Honorable Monk, I am in pursuit of wisdom. I find my mind continuously flustered by worries of the future and remorse of the past. How can I achieve peace?" The Zen Monk, with a half smile gracing his features, picked up a small stone from the ground beside him. Turning his attention back to the boy, he said, "Watch carefully, Yuki." Tossing the stone into the brook, he added, "What do you see?"

Yuki observed the stone cut through the smooth surface of the water, giving life to countless ripples that danced around the center where the stone had disappeared. "Ripples, Monk," the boy replied, a little confused. The Monk turned back to look at the boy, the smile never leaving his face. He nodded gently, signaling that the lesson was not yet over. He asked Yuki to keep observing the water, which was gradually reclaiming its tranquil state.

The conversation between the Monk and the boy ceased momentarily, the only sound being the soft murmur of the flowing brook. The sun continued its descent, casting a warm, golden glow over the scene. Everything felt incredibly peaceful, as if time itself had decided to slow down to savor the moment. However, the most profound part of the lesson was yet to be revealed. As the last ripple faded, leaving the brook once again smooth and undisturbed, the Monk finally spoke. "Yuki, tell me, where are the ripples now?" He asked. Gazing at the tranquil waters, Yuki replied, "They are gone, Monk. They disappeared."

"And so it is with the worries of your mind," the Monk stated softly, maintaining his steady gaze at Yuki. "Just like the ripples, our thoughts about the past and future disturb our present. But if we manage to remain in the present moment, just like this brook, our mind too, will find its way back to tranquility." Yuki listened, the depth of the Monk's words slowly sinking in. Just as the stone had disrupted the brook, his worries and regrets were causing ripples in his mind, disrupting his peace. He needed to allow his mind to return to the present, to the here and now, where it belonged.

"But Monk, how do I bring my mind to rest in the present?" Yuki asked, his voice echoing his yearning for peace. "By embracing the power of presence, Yuki," the Monk stated, his voice as soft as the breeze rustling through the nearby trees. "Focus on the task at hand, on the current moment, on your breath, on the sensation of the wind against your skin or the sounds around you. Bring all your attention to the 'now' and let the ripples of the past and the future fade away."

As the sun dipped below the horizon, Yuki took a deep breath, closing his eyes to truly sense the moment. He could feel the gentle wind, the warmth of the fading sun on his skin, the soft rustle of leaves. In that moment, he truly felt present, the ripples in his mind beginning to fade, replaced by a sense of profound calmness. And in that moment, Yuki understood the power of presence.

40

Tortoise and Hare: The Slow Dance of Patience

igh in the peaceful mountains, between the bamboo groves and tranquil streams, lived a wise Zen monk known as Master Ming. Over time, he had become a revered guide for the village below, sharing his wisdom through enchanting tales, each one containing a profound lesson. One day, a restless youngster named Li Wei approached Master Ming. He was a bright boy, swift in his studies, known for his quick wit and energy, but alas, often depleted of patience. In a world that was always on the run, Li Wei needed to grasp the essence of calm and patience, but it seemed as elusive as the morning mist. Seeing the boy's earnest request, Master Ming smiled gently. He gestured towards the lush valley below, where a tortoise was languidly trailing along a worn path, while a hare darted haphazardly nearby.

"Li Wei," the monk began, his voice as soothing as the mountain breeze, "observe the tortoise and the hare. What do you see?" Li Wei squinted at the scene, watching as the tortoise plodded along, oblivious to the hare's frantic leaps and bounds. "I see the tortoise moving slowly and the hare sprinting ahead, Master."

Master Ming nodded, his eyes sparkling with unspoken wisdom. "Indeed, the hare, with all his speed and agility, dashes forwards, and the tortoise, despite his slow pace, moves steadily along the path. But observe, Li Wei, the rhythm of their dance, the pace of their journey." Li Wei watched, his brow furrowing. He saw the hare's frenetic energy, the frantic leaps, the constant pauses - a dance of fits and starts. He watched the tortoise's unhurried stride, the slow but continuous pace, the determination in every deliberate, unyielding step - the slow, serene dance of patience.

"But Master," Li Wei said, his curiosity piqued, "what does this mean?" Master Ming simply smiled, indicating that the story was far from over. The lesson was yet to unfold, and Li Wei's journey of understanding had only just begun. Master Ming allowed the silence to stretch, to offer his words room to sprout in the boy's mind like a seed in fertile soil. "Patience, Li Wei," he said softly, "is not about being motionless or slow. It is about understanding the rhythm of life, the ebb and flow of time and energy. The hare might cover the ground quickly, but he also exhausts quickly. He is constantly catching his breath, unable to maintain his pace."

Li Wei turned his gaze back to the animals. True to Master Ming's words, the hare lay panting under a tree, while the tortoise, unhurried and unbothered, continued his journey steadily along the path. "In contrast," Master Ming continued, "the tortoise, with his unhurried pace, is persistent. He may be slow, but he is steady. He doesn't rush, nor does he tire. He understands the rhythm of life, the dance of patience. He knows that to reach his destination, he doesn't need to sprint. All he needs is to keep going."

Li Wei watched as the tortoise, slow yet persistent, passed the hare, still panting under the tree. The lesson started to take root in his heart. The monk gently laid his hand on Li Wei's shoulder. "In life, Li Wei," he said, "one must learn the dance of the tortoise. Success isn't about who is the fastest or the strongest, but who can maintain their rhythm till the end. Patience isn't the inability to take action; it's the ability to stay steady, to keep going, even when the world around you is in haste."

Li Wei, his eyes still locked on the tortoise, felt a sense of calm wash over him. The hare might have speed, but the tortoise had something greater - wisdom and patience. As he watched the tortoise's slow dance of patience, Li Wei, like a sapling stretching towards sunlight, felt himself grow. And therein, the lesson unfolded, not in words, but experience. The slow dance of patience had begun.

41

Moth's Flirt with Flame: Temptations and Balance

Once upon a time in a serene monastery in the emerald green mountains and the azure sky, there lived an old monk named Zihan. His abode was the temple's meditation hall, a space filled with tranquility, and adorned with ancient scrolls and the faint aroma of sandalwood incense. One night, as Zihan sat meditating, a tiny moth fluttered into the room. Drawn by the only source of light, a dimly lit butter lamp, the moth circled around it in a display of fascinating dance. The old monk opened an eye and watched as the moth dived toward the flame, only to be pushed back by the searing heat. Yet, it returned again and again, flirting perilously with the bright dancing flame.

The moth's behavior intrigued Zihan. He noticed the moth's relentless pursuit despite the evident danger. An almost perfect symbolism for human temptations and desires, he mused. Just as the moth was drawn to the flame, despite its deadly nature, human beings were lured by the glitter and glamour of worldly pleasures despite knowing their potential to harm or distract us from our spiritual path. Zihan's gaze followed the moth as it undertook its hypnotic dance once more. A sense of sadness seeped into him as he anticipated the moth's fate. Nevertheless, he continued to observe, aware that life often unfolded its mysteries in the most ordinary events.

The night deepened, and the moth's dance with the flame continued. As the wind whispered through the trees, Zihan lowered his meditative gaze to the flickering flame and the moth playing its dangerous game of balance with the irresistible, yet destructive light.

As moments passed into hours, the moth's energy began to wane. Its movements became less vigorous, its attempts at reaching the flame less frequent. Yet, its eyes never left the hypnotic dance of the flame, even as it rested on the rim of the butter lamp. Zihan, considering the moth's plight, realized the important lesson it offered. Like the moth, humans too become entrapped in the seductive dance of earthly desires, losing their energy and zeal for life in the process.

Taking a deep breath, Zihan decided to intervene. He gently picked up the moth and placed it on the window sill, away from the butter lamp. The moth, initially disoriented, soon fluttered its wings and took off into the cool night. As Zihan watched the moth disappear into the darkness, he felt a profound sense of peace and understanding. Just like he had helped the moth escape its dangerous fascination, humans too could be guided away from their destructive desires. They could find balance between the temptations of the world and their spiritual path.

This realization reinforced his belief in his mission as a Zen monk - to help others recognize their patterns of desire, to guide them towards understanding, and to show them how to find serenity amidst the chaos of life. He returned to his meditation with a renewed sense of purpose, the flickering flame now a symbol of wisdom and enlightenment rather than temptation and destruction.

The night deepened further and as the first rays of dawn crept into the meditation hall, Zihan sat in contemplative silence, reassured and enlightened. The image of the moth, liberated from its destructive dance, served as a powerful reminder of the delicate balance between desire and spiritual growth. And as the morning sun rose, the wisdom it brought blossomed within him, ready to be shared with those who sought it.

42

Harp Strings in a Silent Space: Echoes of Emptiness

In a remote mountain village in ancient Japan, there once lived a gifted musician named Hiroshi. His talent with a koto, a traditional Japanese stringed instrument, was unparalleled. He played with such beauty and grace that every note seemed to bloom into life, filling the quiet mountain air with an enchanting melody. People from far and wide would travel to hear Hiroshi's soul-stirring compositions. One day, a Zen monk named Kazuki, known for his profound wisdom and serenity, came to the village. He had heard tales of Hiroshi's extraordinary talent and wished to experience it for himself. Kazuki was well-versed in the teachings of Zen, a school of Mahayana Buddhism that emphasized wisdom through meditation and insight. He believed that music was a tangible form of this wisdom and wished to see if Hiroshi's music could provide an insight of its own.

That evening, Hiroshi sat before his koto with Kazuki amongst the audience. As his fingers began to dance across the strings, a mesmerizing melody filled the air, resonating with the hearts of those who listened. However, as the performance continued, Hiroshi noticed the monk's unmoved expression. Looking at Kazuki's peaceful countenance, Hiroshi felt a rising sense of challenge. He began playing his most intricate composition, a melody that had brought the most stoic of samurais to tears. As the final note echoed into silence, the audience erupted into applause. But once again, Monk Kazuki remained still, his face a mask of tranquility. Confused and a little frustrated, Hiroshi approached the monk.

"Why do you not applaud my music, monk? Does it not move you?" Hiroshi asked, his voice laced with a hint of irritation. Kazuki smiled slightly, his eyes reflecting the calmness of a still lake, "Your music is indeed beautiful, Hiroshi," he said. "But I am searching for something more. I want to hear the music in the silence that follows. The echoes of emptiness, if you will."

Hiroshi looked at the monk, perplexed, not fully understanding the depth of Kazuki's words. After all, how could silence be music? Little did he know, this strange encounter with the monk would lead him to a profound realization. In the days that followed, Hiroshi found himself wrestling with Monk Kazuki's words. He would sit for hours before his koto, plucking at the strings, then pausing to listen to the ensuing silence. Yet the more he searched, the more elusive the 'echoes of emptiness' became.

One afternoon, as he sat in frustrated silence, a gentle breeze rustled through the cherry blossom trees, carrying with it a soft, musical sound. He watched as the petals swirled and twinkled against the vibrant blue sky, falling gently on his koto. The sight was breathtaking, and a lightness filled his heart. It was then Hiroshi realized it. He had been so focused on the music he created, he had overlooked the natural symphony around him. The rustling leaves, the chirping birds, the gurgling stream - all were sounds that echoed in emptiness, yet were full of life and harmony. Even the silence after his music held its own melody, a continuation of the story he had begun with his koto's strings.

With this newfound understanding, Hiroshi once again sat before his koto. This time, he played not to impress, but to express. He played not only the notes but the silences in between. He played his koto as an extension of nature's orchestra, weaving a melody that moved seamlessly from his strings to the echoes of emptiness. When he finished, he found Monk Kazuki in the audience, his face now reflecting a deep, radiant joy. "Ah, Hiroshi, you have found it," he said, clasping the musician's hands. "The echoes of emptiness now sing through your music, bringing with it a profound depth of wisdom, as enlightening as the teachings of Zen."

From that day forward, Hiroshi's music embodied a harmonious blend of sound and silence, earning him a new, elevated reverence amongst his listeners. As for Hiroshi himself, he played with a sense of fulfillment and joy, knowing he was part of the symphony of life, resonating with the echoes of emptiness.

43

Zen Gardener and Hidden Blooms: Trust in Unseen Growth

𝓘n a small village on the outskirts of ancient Kyoto, there lived a wise, old Zen Monk known for his serenity and deep understanding of life's mysteries. For decades, he had tended to a humble Zen garden, a silent oasis filled with meticulously raked sands, rocks, and elite, carefully pruned trees. But at the heart of his garden, lay a patch of barren soil which seemed nothing more than an anomaly in his otherwise flawless paradise. One gloomy winter day, a young village lad, unable to contain his curiosity, respectfully approached the old monk. "Honored one," he inquired with a bow, "Why do you keep this barren patch in your beautiful garden? It only seems to dull the magnificence of the rest."

The old monk simply smiled, his eyes twinkling with a secret wisdom. "Patience, young one," he said, "This patch of soil is more than what it appears." Intrigued, the boy visited frequently over the following weeks, but the patch remained as barren as ever. The monk continued cultivating the earth, watering it, and caring for it with the same diligence as the resplendent parts of his garden. The boy couldn't help but feel a pang of disappointment each time he saw the monk working the barren patch with unwavering devotion.

As weeks turned into months, the winter snow melted away to welcome the first signs of spring. The boy, now a regular visitor to the Monk's garden, arrived one day to find the monk sitting peacefully by the barren patch, his eyes reflecting the soft morning sunlight. The boy's heart sank in confusion as he looked over at the unchanged soil. "But Master," he said, his voice wavering with exasperation, "There is still no bloom. There is only the same unyielding earth."

"Look closer, my child," the Zen monk repeated gently, his gaze unwavering from the patch. The boy knelt beside him, his eyes scrupulously scanning the plot of dirt, not understanding what the monk wanted him to observe. But, as he was about to express his confusion, he saw it. A tiny bud, barely visible, had pierced through the soil. "It...it is a sprout!" the boy exclaimed, his eyes wide with surprise and wonder. The monk nodded, a warm smile playing on his lips. "In our lives, there are many things that don't reveal their magnificence at first glance. Some things need time, care, and patience to bloom in their own time." The boy looked at the new green life, then back at the monk with a dawning understanding. The monk continued, "This patch of earth taught me a splendid lesson. Even if it appeared barren, under my care and patience, it finally showed its hidden potential."

Days passed, and the boy continued visiting. He watched as the sprout grew into a flowering plant, spreading its vibrancy in the otherwise barren patch. The monk's persevering care and faith had allowed the plant to thrive, turning the barren land into a symbol of growth and resilience. As the plant blossomed, so did the boy's understanding. He learned to trust the unseen growth, to understand that not all progress is instantly visible and that patience, care, and faith can transform even a barren land into a flourishing garden.

The Zen monk's wisdom had once again breathed life into a barren patch, not only of his garden but also into the young boy's understanding. The monk's garden truly was a reflection of life itself, teaching lessons of patience, trust, and unseen growth.

44

Rainbows Born of Rain: Beauty After Struggles

Once upon a time, in a quiet village in the heart of a lush valley, there lived an old, wise monk named Soto. He had a reputation for possessing an unshakeable tranquility, even in the face of the most trying circumstances. One day, the serene blue sky suddenly turned a somber gray, and a storm began to brew over the village. It was not just a brief shower; it was a relentless torrent that seemed as if it would not cease. The villagers were disheartened and worried as their lush green fields were flooded and crops were in danger of being ruined. The usual hustle and bustle of the village gave way to a grim silence, punctuated only by the steady falling of rain.

Despite this, Soto maintained his calm demeanor and continued his daily routines. He chanted his prayers, swept the monastery grounds, and meditated under the Bodhi tree with his eyes closed, seemingly unaffected by the downpour. The villagers passing by him couldn't help but feel a sense of awe at Soto's tranquility in the midst of the storm. During one day, as the hard rain was falling, a young boy from the village approached Soto. He stood, soaked to the bone, staring at the monk with wide curious eyes. He finally gathered the courage to ask the question that was bothering him.

"Master Soto," he began, his voice barely audible over the pouring rain, "why are you not upset like the others?" He gestured towards the village, "Our crops are drowning, our homes are leaking, and yet you sit here so peacefully. Don't you realize the harshness of this storm?" Soto opened his eyes and looked at the young boy. A faint smile tugged at the corners of his mouth. With a calm voice, he replied, "Young one, have you ever seen a rainbow?"

The boy, confused by the monk's response, looked at him puzzled. Before he could utter a response, Soto continued, his eyes reflecting the wisdom of the ages. "Yes, Master Soto. I've seen many rainbows. They're beautiful," the boy replied, still confused by the connection. Soto nodded, his gaze momentarily shifting towards the rain-soaked village. "A rainbow, young one, is formed only after a storm. It's a beautiful spectacle, born out of the sky's turmoil. It's a sign of hope, a promise of better times ahead. But it only graces us after the rain has drenched the earth."

The boy stood silent, taking in the monk's words. Soto then turned back to face the rain. "Just like the storm that's causing us discomfort now, life too, often brings challenges. They may be daunting, even destructive. Yet it's only through these trials that we grow, learn, and discover our strengths. Like the rainbow after the storm, brighter days come only after we've weathered the squall. We must endure with patience and hope." Soto's voice was soft, yet his words resonated with a profound wisdom that silenced even the storm. The boy's eyes widened in understanding, his fear and worry giving way to a sense of calm.

As if on cue, the rain began to lessen, the gray clouds slowly parting to reveal a magnificent rainbow arching across the sky. The villagers, who had been listening from their doorsteps, were filled with awe at the sight, their faces reflecting the colors of hope and resilience. The boy looked at Soto, his eyes gleaming in gratitude. He didn't say a word, but Soto knew he had understood. The monk closed his eyes again, a serene smile playing on his lips. Amidst the turmoil, he had helped another soul discover the beauty after struggles, just like the rainbows born of rain.

As the village slowly returned to its usual hustle and bustle, a newfound resilience breathed life into its heart, a silent reminder of the wisdom shared under the Bodhi tree. A whispering wind carried the lesson onwards, to whoever was ready to listen and learn.

45

Quill's Pause:
The Potential of Pause

Quill, a young monk, was known for his tireless commitment to his practice. Hours transformed into days, days into weeks, and still, he remained undeterred in his pursuit of enlightenment. From the breaking of dawn to the arrival of twilight, Quill could be found in the monastery's temple, his silhouette silhouetted against the backdrop of tranquility. One day, Master Zhen noticed Quill's unwavering dedication. His gaze lingered on the young monk, observing his relentless focus, and the rhythmic rise and fall of his chest as he breathed life into the stillness. "Quill," Master Zhen finally called out, pulling the young monk from his intense focus.

"Yes, Master," Quill replied, his eyes still closed, his hands folded gently in front of him. "I've watched you for many weeks now," Master Zhen began. "Your dedication is admirable, your focus, unparalleled. But I've noticed that you rarely pause. You are always in motion, always pushing forward in your spiritual quest." Quill opened his eyes at this, a frown creasing his youthful face. "But Master," he protested, "isn't that the point? To keep striving for enlightenment, to keep moving forward?"

Master Zhen responded with a soft smile, his wise eyes gleaming in the soft candlelight. "True wisdom, Quill, is not just about forward momentum, but also about the ability to be still and to pause." Quill's frown deepened. He was young, passionate, eager to attain enlightenment. Every moment not spent in focused meditation seemed like a wasted opportunity. He was on a journey, an unstoppable train hurdling towards its destination. A pause? It seemed foreign, even counterproductive to Quill. But he respected his Master, and so, with a sigh, he decided to embrace this new challenge. Any wisdom that seemed counter-intuitive was often the most profound. After all, he was but a humble student.

With a nod of acknowledgment, Quill rose from his lotus position, his heart heavy with uncertainty. Could he really discover something valuable in the silence of a pause? He was about to find out. And with that, he embarked on a new journey – the journey of learning to pause. In the following days, Quill attempted to put Master Zhen's advice in practice. He tried to infuse pauses into his day, interspersing his relentless pursuit of knowledge with moments of stillness. But each time he sat idle, his mind rebelled against the silence, thoughts whirling like leaves in a tempest. There was a restlessness in him, a hunger that was never satiated. Master Zhen observed Quill's struggles and finally one day, he invited Quill to accompany him to the monastery's garden. Basking in the quietude, the Master picked up a blossoming flower, gently handling its delicate petals.

"Do you see this flower, Quill?" Master Zhen asked. Quill nodded, unsure where this was leading. "Each day, it opens up a little more, absorbing the sunlight, drinking the morning dew. It doesn't rush to blossom all at once. Instead, it pauses, it rests, allowing nature to nurture it at its own pace." Master Zhen's eyes met Quill's, "Can you apply this wisdom to your journey to enlightenment?"

The essence of the Master's message pierced through the cloud of Quill's confusion. Suddenly, he understood. The pause was not about halting progress. It was about acknowledging the present, understanding its importance, and allowing it to shape the journey.

Embracing this revelation, Quill began to change. His practices were no longer a race towards enlightenment but a harmonious blend of motion and pause. With each well-timed halt, Quill found himself feeling more grounded, more attuned to the world around him, and oddly enough, closer to the enlightenment he sought. In the wisdom of the pause, Quill found a new rhythm to life. It seemed that Master Zhen was right all along. The potential was indeed in the pause. Through its tranquility, Quill was discovering his path to enlightenment at a pace that was uniquely his, crafting a journey where every step and every stop held equal significance.

46

Giant's Lessons from an Ant: Relative Strengths

*J*n the shadowy folds of the Daitokuji Mountain range, a Zen monk known as Master Kodo lived in a humble wooden hermitage, surrounded by nature's grandness and serenity. One radiant morning, as he was meditating by the sparkling creek, he noticed a strange sight. A small ant struggled to carry a large leaf across the pebbled path. Despite the leaf being much larger than itself, the ant persisted with unwavering resolve. Master Kodo paused his meditation and watched the ant's diligent efforts with keen interest. The ant moved one step at a time, pushing itself forward. Sometimes it would stumble and lose grip, but it always crawled back and resumed the effort soon after.

That very afternoon, a giant lumbered into the peaceful solitude of the hermitage. His colossal body shook the earth with every step. His name was Dai, a nomad who traveled across the Land of the Rising Sun. Dai had heard of Master Kodo's wisdom, so he sought him out to seek guidance for an issue that troubled him deeply.

"I am the strongest in all the land, yet I feel weak, Master," Dai confessed in a voice as deep as a rumbling storm. "Even the slightest emotional disturbance cripples me, and I find myself unable to wield my strength properly." Master Kodo, looking at Dai, remembered the ant from the morning. "Come sit with me by the creek, Dai," he said, signaling towards a moss-covered stone adjacent to his. He shared no words after that, but his eyes twinkled with the onset of a lesson.

As Dai lumbered behind him, his mind was filled with curiosity. He wondered how sitting by a creek would address his struggle. His large frame cast a dark shadow across the serene landscape, contrasting sharply with the tranquility of the creek. Master Kodo began to speak, but his words were aimed at the ant and not at the giant. For amidst Nature's wonders, the Monk found a lesson echoing in the determination of the smallest creature, a lesson potentially large enough to enlighten the giant.

"Dai," began Master Kodo, "Observe this ant." His voice was soft yet steady, like the murmur of the creek beside them. Dai squinted down at the pebbled path, his eyes finally resting on the tiny ant. He watched as it struggled with a leaf much larger than itself, yet it continued to press on. "This ant," Master Kodo continued, "is much smaller than you. It does not possess your physical strength, yet it carries a burden much larger than its size. It stumbles, yet it persists. Each step it takes, regardless of how small, carries it closer to its goal."

Dai observed the ant in silence, his eyes reflecting a newfound understanding. "It is not the strength of the body, but the resilience of the spirit," he murmured, his deep voice echoing the wisdom of the monk.

"Exactly," Master Kodo replied, a gentle smile playing on his lips. "Your physical strength may be colossal, yet it is your emotional strength that needs honing. Like the ant, you must learn not to be deterred by the size of your challenges, but to persist, one step at a time."

Dai looked at the ant, his gaze softening. He then turned to Master Kodo, humility replacing the confusion in his eyes. The monk's words had cleared his mind, casting a new light on his struggles. From that day forth, Dai no longer saw his emotions as a hindrance to his strength. He understood that they were a part of him, a testament to his human nature, not a flaw that needed to be eradicated. And like the ant, he learned to carry his emotional burdens with grace, one step at a time. This newfound wisdom transformed him from a mere giant into a true titan, resilient in spirit and mighty in heart. The ant's lesson, as small and seemingly insignificant as it was, had blossomed a profound wisdom within the heart of the giant.

47

The Song Once Lost, Now Found: Reviving Joy

Once upon a time, in the calmer hours of a peaceful Japanese village, lived a Zen monk known for his wisdom and perpetual tranquility. This monk, named Master Akira, resided in a humble abode near the azure water of the Ikemori river, embraced by the lush landscape of cherry blossom trees. One spring afternoon, as Master Akira ambled along the riverbank, a subtle melancholic note caught his ear, disrupting the symphony of nature. It was the sound of a distant shamisen, a traditional Japanese instrument, playing a tune soaked in sorrow. Intrigued and ever compassionate, Master Akira followed the melancholic melody to its source.

He discovered a young woman named Hanako by the river, her fingers strumming the strings of her shamisen with a practiced touch. Her eyes were sorrowful, heavy with tears unshed, the melancholy in her music reflecting her inner turmoil. She paused her playing as she noticed the monk and offered him a slight bow. "Forgive me, Master Akira," she began, her voice barely more than a whisper, "I did not mean to disturb your peace with my music."

Master Akira returned the bow and gestured for her to continue. "No disturbance, Hanako-san. A melody, serene or sorrowful, is a reflection of the heart," he said, his gaze compassionate. "I sense a deep pain in your melody, a joy once held, now lost." Hanako nodded, her gaze lowered. "Indeed, Master Akira. Once, my shamisen brought joy, painted the air with melodies of happiness. But since my mother passed, I seem to have lost that joy. My music, it feels muted, as if a part of it has died with her."

Master Akira listened to her with empathy, understanding the loss that shadowed her heart. In the silence that followed, he pondered the nature of joy and loss, the beautiful memory of a song once alive, and the melancholy of a song now muted. Master Akira broke the silence, "Hanako, life is an unending cycle of birth, growth, decay, and renewal. Your sorrow is but a testament to the love and joy that your mother brought into your life. Let not her passing mute the joy in your music, but enrich it."

"But Master Akira, how can I play a joyous melody when my heart is so heavy?" asked Hanako, her eyes seeking answers. The monk gave a knowing smile, "Hanako-san, you're holding onto your sorrow too tightly, trying to find your joy in the past. You're playing the song of an echo, trying to capture the melody that your mother once loved. But the joy you seek is not in the past, but in the present, in the melody you have yet to play."

"But how can I find joy without my mother?" Hanako asked. "By cherishing the joy she brought into your life," Master Akira advised, "Take that joy, and weave it into your melody. Your mother might not be here in form, but in spirit, she is all around us. Each note you play is a tribute to her. Let her spirit inspire your melody. Revive your joy by embracing the wisdom of her love." Hanako's eyes sparkled with newfound understanding, a hint of a smile playing on her lips. She picked up her shamisen, her fingers dancing on the strings. And as she played, a new melody filled the air. It was not just a melody of sorrow but one of love, acceptance, and joy. It was a song once lost, now found.

Master Akira, listening to the newfound joy in Hanako's music, remained silently by the riverside as the soft spring breeze rustled the cherry blossoms. The river flowed gently, mirroring the journey of life - ever changing, ever renewing, ever flowing. The song once lost was now found, and with it, the joy that Hanako thought she had lost forever.

48

Flowers at Volcano's Feet:
Life's Contrasts

The Zen monk, Master Shōnin, journeyed with his young disciple, Hideo, through a region known for its active volcano. Hideo, energetic and curious, had been pestering his master with questions about the purpose of their journey to such a dangerous place.

"Why are we here, Master?" Hideo asked, fear and excitement playing in his eyes as they neared the fiery mountain. Master Shōnin, it seemed, was waiting for just this question. He pointed towards the base of the volcano, where a burst of color flourished against the stark, ash-gray landscape. "Look there, Hideo." His finger directed the young monk's gaze to a field of resplendent azaleas, their vibrant blossoms undeterred by the volcano's ominous presence. These beautiful flowers, defying nature's adversity, had found a way to thrive in the shadow of destruction. It was a spectacle that held Hideo spellbound, his young mind grappling with the strange coexistence of beauty and danger, life and potential death.

Witnessing Hideo's wonder, Master Shōnin smiled, his eyes mirroring the warm, orange glow of the volcano's heart. The impending lesson, he knew, would be a profound one for his disciple, a lesson of contrasts, one that would take root and blossom within Hideo, much like the flowers at the volcano's feet. The scene was set, and the story ripe for the telling. The master knew that the coming dialogue would shape not only Hideo's understanding of life and its inherent challenges, but also his capacity for resilience and adaptation in the face of adversity.

Like the volcano and the flowers, Master Shōnin and Hideo were contrasts themselves - the old and the young, wisdom and innocence - united in a singular journey, in a quest of enlightenment under an indigo sky. Together, as the sun began to set, casting long, dramatic shadows across the terrain, they set forth towards the field of azaleas, towards the wisdom waiting to be unfurled. They moved closer to the field of azaleas, their steps slow and thoughtful, matching the rhythm of the earth beneath their feet. The air was warm, filled with the comforting scent of the blossoms and a hint of volcanic ash. It was an unusual but not unpleasant mix, a testament to the peculiar charm of life's contrasts.

"Life, Hideo," Master Shōnin began, keeping his gaze on the flowers, "is full of contradictions. But, in these contradictions, there lies wisdom. Observe these azaleas. They grow not despite the volcano, but because of it." Hideo's brows furrowed in thought. "Isn't the volcano dangerous, Master?"

"Yes, it is," replied the monk, a soft chuckle escaping his lips. "Much like life itself. It holds the power of destruction and creation in the same hand. The same volcanic soil that threatens to bury life also nurtures it. The azaleas draw strength from the ash, their beauty is a testament to adversity faced and overcome." Hideo's eyes widened with newfound understanding. He seemed to view the flowers anew, their vibrant hues telling a story of resilience and hope. "Adversity, Hideo, is the soil in which courage blossoms. Just as these azaleas thrive at the volcano's feet, so too can we flourish in the face of difficulties. The choice is in how we perceive and respond to the challenges that life presents."

As the sun set, the volcano's glow provided the only illumination, casting an ethereal light on the field of azaleas. The scene was a painting of life's paradoxes - destruction and creation, fear and courage, despair and hope. It was a lesson Hideo would carry with him, a lesson in embracing life's contrasts and finding beauty amidst adversity.

Later that night, as Hideo drifted to sleep to the rhythm of the earth's heartbeat, the wisdom of the day bloomed in his heart, promising a life of courage, resilience, and understanding, much like the blossoming azaleas at the feet of the volcano.

49

Sun and Shade's Dance: Embracing Life's Dualities

nder the warm afternoon sun, an old Zen Monk named Ryoan, sat quietly in the courtyard of his weathered monastery. Squinting beneath the tranquil sky, his eyes traced the vibrant cherry blossom tree that stood resolute in the heart of the space. One could not help but notice the stark contrast between the sun's radiant glow and the tree's soothing shade. Ryoan had watched this tree for decades. The seasons flowed around it like a river around a rock, yet it persisted. It blossomed under the spring sun, bore fruit in the summer, lost leaves in the fall, and stood bare in winter's frost. Sun and shade, heat and cold, life and death, the tree experienced it all with an enduring grace. Before him, two young disciples, Naoki and Ren, were engaged in a lively debate. "Surely," exclaimed Naoki, "the sun is more important, for it nourishes the tree, allows the flowers to bloom, and brings life to all creatures."

"No," countered Ren, "it is the shade that is crucial. It offers protection from the harsh summer sun and provides us with a peaceful space for quiet contemplation." Listening quietly, Ryoan smiled to himself. He understood the instinct to view life in terms of a singular, prevailing influence. Yet, it was the complexities of dichotomies, the dance between the sun and shade, that constituted the true rhythm of existence.

He called out to his disciples, "Naoki, Ren, join me under this cherry blossom tree." As the two disciples came into the shade, Ryoan looked at the tree and then at the sun playing peek-a-boo behind the branches. His eyes twinkled as he prepared to share his wisdom, a wisdom nurtured by the interplay of sun and shade, of life's beautiful dualities. As the disciples settled beside him, Ryoan gestured towards the cherry blossom tree, its branches swaying gently in the breeze, caught in a celestial ballet of light and shadow. "Naoki, Ren," he began, "this tree, our silent companion, doesn't ask the sun to shine brighter or the shade to deepen. It accepts both as they come, taking what it needs from each. Just as it stands tall in full sun, it equally relishes the relief of shade."

Ryoan picked up a fallen blossom, turning it carefully in his hand. "Naoki, you see in the sun a force of life, of nourishment. And you are correct. Yet if the sun shone relentlessly without night's respite or cloud's cover, it would scorch the earth, fading the beauty it once nurtured." Ryoan then pointed at the long shadow cast by the monastery wall, a cool blanket of solitude. "And Ren, you see in the shade a realm of peace, of protection. Indeed it is. But continuous shadow breeds stagnation, stifles growth. It is the sun's journey across the sky that gives birth to the shade you value."

Gazing at the two disciples, Ryoan continued, "Life's beauty emerges from this dance between the sun and the shade, between opposing forces. It's about embracing the warmth and the cool, the light and the dark, the joy and the sorrow. Each one is incomplete without the other, each one gives the other meaning."

As the afternoon gave way to dusk, Ryoan's words echoed in the tranquil courtyard. The monk, the disciples, the cherry blossom tree, they all sat in silence, basking in the fading sun and the deepening shade. In the dance of these dualities, they discovered an understanding, a blossoming wisdom: the art of embracing life as it is, not as they desired it to be.

50

Child's Gaze upon Fleeting Bubbles: Transient Beauty

The Zen Monk sat cross-legged in the lush verdant garden, eyes closed in deep contemplation, yet acutely aware of the vibrancy of life around him. The soft rustle of the wind in the bamboo leaves, the twittering of distant birds, and the occasional chuckling gurgle of the nearby brook set a melody that harmonized with the tranquil stillness of his soul. By his side, a tad separated from his serenity, was a young boy, the Monk's novice, engrossed in his own world of adventure. In contrast to the Monk, the boy's lit eyes followed a soap bubble he had just blown into existence, giggling as it danced on the gentle wind before finally bursting into nothingness. The boy clapped with delight and blew another bubble, laughing as the process repeated itself.

Breaking from his meditation, the Zen Monk peeked an eye open, observing the boy's innocent fascination with the bubbles. His gaze traced each bubble's journey, from its genesis into a colorful sphere, up until its inevitable return to being a mere drop of water, a cycle of life and death played out in a simple child's game. Awe and anticipation filled the boy's eyes as he watched the life of each bubble, never knowing when or where they would pop, yet finding joy in their fleeting existence. Every bubble held a different path, a unique dance pattern on the breeze, a different lifespan before its end. Yet, the boy rejoiced in all of them, and even in their burst, he would cheerfully create another, his laughter echoing the bubbles' iridescent beauty.

The Monk watched, a warm smile etched on his face, the boy's innocent joy resonating with his own wisdom-infused serenity. Here, in this moment, in the simple act of a child blowing bubbles, the Monk saw the transient nature of life, of beauty, of joy, and of sorrow painted vividly. Yet, like the young boy, he too, was engrossed, not in the bubbles, but in the raw, joyful curiosity reflected in the child's gaze. In the sound of his novice's laughter, the Monk heard the echo of his own journey from innocence to enlightenment; a journey marked by a multitude of 'bubbles' burst too soon, and yet, each contributing to his understanding of the world. His fingers brushed over the cool grass beneath him, each blade a reminder of the transient beauty all around.

With a soft chuckle, the Monk turned to the boy, "What do you see in that bubble, young one?" he asked, his voice as gentle as the evening breeze. The boy, his cheeks red with exertion and joy, looked up at the Monk, "A bubble, Master!" he exclaimed, eyes sparkling with excitement. He then eagerly blew another bubble into existence, his gaze hitching onto it as it danced away on their shared breath. A patient smile spread across the Monk's face. "Look again," He encouraged, gesturing toward the iridescent orb floating by.

The boy squinted, his little brow furrowing before his face lit up, "I see...colors, Master! Like a tiny rainbow." The Monk nodded, "Indeed. And what happens when the bubble bursts?"

"It's gone," answered the boy, a hint of sadness creeping into his twinkle, "Just like that." "And do you mourn for it?" asked the Monk, watching the boy. "No," the boy shook his head, his eyes keen on the Monk, "I just make another." The Monk's smile widened, his heart warmed by the wisdom blooming in the young novice. "Much like the bubbles, life too, is transient, delicate, and vibrantly beautiful. And like you, when faced with loss, we too must learn to create joy anew, to embrace the burst as not an end, but the beginning of another beautiful dance."

The boy's eyes widened before a wide smile spread across his face, a deeper understanding dawning upon him. He turned back to his game, his laughter carrying a new note of wisdom, filling the garden with the sound of the blossoming joy.

51

Butterfly's Break from Chains: Liberation from Limitations

In the quaint village in the verdant mountains, there lived a simple Zen monk named Sho. He had an uninterrupted routine that revolved around meditation, mindful living, and the inhabitants of his beautiful Zen garden. The garden was home to verdant greens, blossoming flowers, and countless living creatures, each with their own unique stories. The most captivating one was that of a small, seemingly insignificant caterpillar named Hoshi. Unlike other caterpillars, Hoshi was not content with her existence. She was encumbered by her inability to ascend to the vast skies and explore the world beyond the garden. Amidst the fluttering butterflies, chirping birds, and floating clouds, her world was limited to crawling on the earth and nibbling on leaves. Her dreams, however, soared higher than the tallest tree in the Zen garden.

One day, as the radiant sun illuminated the Zen garden, Hoshi was found by Sho tangled in a maze of twigs and fallen leaves. The little caterpillar shared her aspirations with the kind monk, expressing her longing to break free from her physical constraints and explore the world above. Sho listened attentively, observing the caterpillar's frustration mirrored in the unchecked tears that carved streaks down her soft face. Sho, though moved, expressed neither pity nor comfort. Instead, he offered Hoshi a warm smile, "The universe," he began gently, "has a unique plan for all of us. Sometimes, our present circumstances are but a part of a grand scheme that we are yet to comprehend."

That night, as the moon bathed the garden in its soothing luminescence, Hoshi couldn't help but gaze at the twinkling stars. She yearned for the freedom they promised, the liberation she dreamt of. But for now, she was but a caterpillar in a Zen monk's garden, wishing upon a star. The universe was silent, and Hoshi couldn't shake the feeling that her dreams would forever remain just that—dreams. Days turned into weeks, and the incessant tick of time did nothing to dampen Hoshi's dreams. The humble Zen garden was a canvas of changes, with the fall leaves painting it in a myriad of hues; yet, Hoshi felt trapped in a monochrome world. Every attempt to climb the towering trees ended in a discouraging fall, and each passing butterfly was a bitter reminder of her unfulfilled dreams.

One day, a crippling fatigue took over Hoshi. She could no longer bear the weight of her dreams and the constant disappointment. She felt heavy, so she secluded herself inside a tight cocoon, surrendering to the overwhelming exhaustion. The garden continued with its harmonious symphony, oblivious to Hoshi's isolation. Meanwhile, Sho was observing Hoshi with mindful awareness. He recognized the cocoon stage as an important phase of an impending transition, a move towards the unknown. Not once did he seek to expedite or interfere with the natural process.

When the day of liberation finally arrived, it was a regular morning. Sho, unfolding his daily routine, sauntered through the garden, and he noticed the cocoon was split open. A wave of excitement washed over him, and there, perched delicately on the leaf where the cocoon once was, was a beautiful butterfly. Hoshi had transformed. Her once limited world had now expanded, vibrant with colors and endless skies. She was no longer a prisoner of her physical constraints. The earth below became the foundation of her past, and the sky was her new abode.

With newfound freedom, Hoshi soared above the Zen garden, her wings sparkling under the sun's benevolent gaze. Sho watched, a sense of fulfillment nestled within him. The once desperate caterpillar was now a symbol of liberation blooming with newfound wisdom. The universe had answered Hoshi's cries, not by fulfilling her wishes instantly but by guiding her through a journey of self-growth and transformation.

52

Chants in the Valley: Amplifying Positivity

Once upon a time, in the serene valleys of the Himachal, lived a reticent Zen monk named Fugai. He lived in a modest wooden shack, at the foot of the majestic Himalayas. Every morning, as the first rays of the sun kissed the snow-capped peaks, Fugai would step outside, seating himself on a flat, smooth stone with the valley spread out beneath him. As he sat enveloped by the silence of the dawn, he felt the warm sun on his face, the cool breeze playing with his robe, and the expansive valley breathing life into the world. One fine morning, Fugai decided to bring a change in his routine. Instead of his usual silent meditation, he chose to chant. As the mantra echoed through the valley, nature seemed to listen attentively. Birds circled overhead, chirping in sync, the river flowing through the valley hummed along, and the wind whispered the mantra as it passed through the trees.

A few weeks passed, and the valley began to transform. The grass seemed greener, flowers were blooming in abundance, and birds of vivid hues flocked from distant lands. The river flowed with a newfound vitality, and the trees stood taller, swaying rhythmically in the wind. Down in the village, people started noticing this transformation. They saw the once barren valley flourishing with life. Curiosity led them to Fugai's humble abode. From atop his stone seat, Fugai saw a group of villagers approaching, led by the village elder, a wise man named Bodhi. As they reached him, Bodhi asked with a sense of wonder, "Fugai, what magic have you performed on this valley?"

Fugai simply smiled and began to explain that the change was not wrought by magic, but by something far more profound. However, before he could continue, a strong gust of wind swept through the valley, carrying the monk's chants along with it. The villagers looked at each other, their eyes filled with curiosity and anticipation for what was to come.

Fugai parted his lips and replied in his soft voice, "It's not magic, dear Bodhi. It is the power of positivity, amplified by the chants. The continuous repetition of the mantra has created a wave of positive energy that has enveloped the valley."

The villagers whispered among themselves, trying to comprehend the profound words uttered by the monk. Sensing their confusion, Fugai added, "Our thoughts are like seeds. Plant negativity, and it'll grow into a thorny bush. However, plant positivity, and it'll bloom like these lovely flowers around us. The chants are seeds of positivity that I've been sowing into the valley." One of the villagers, a young boy named Aman, timidly asked, "Can we also learn the mantra?" Fugai nodded, his eyes twinkling with joy at the eager curiosity of the young one.

The next morning, the villagers gathered around Fugai on the hilltop. The cool air was tinged with an aura of anticipation. As Fugai started his chant, the villagers followed suit. The valley once again rang with the harmonious echo of their voices, magnifying the positivity that Fugai had cultivated. With time, not just the valley, but the villagers too transformed. They worked with newfound enthusiasm and joy, their hearts and minds brimming with positivity. Conflicts diminished, and a sense of unity prevailed among them.

One day, an outsider visited the village. Seeing the vibrancy and camaraderie amongst the villagers, he was intrigued. On asking about the secret to their happiness, Bodhi pointed towards the hilltop where Fugai sat chanting, and said, "It was not some magic. It was the power of positivity that we learned from Fugai."

The story of the chanting monk and his blossoming wisdom spread, inspiring many more to embrace positivity, thus creating a wave of joy, peace, and prosperity in the world around them.

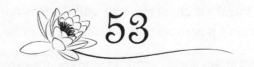

53

Monk's Dance with Shadows: Accepting Impermanence

$\mathcal{I}$n the secluded village of Qi-lin, in the majestic mountains of southern China, lived a Zen monk named Master Shen. Known for his radiant wisdom and tranquility, he was a beacon of light for the villagers. However, his serenity was challenged one day when the most vibrant cherry blossom tree in the monastery's garden started withering. Despite his best efforts to nurture it back to health, the tree's condition worsened by the day. During one sunny afternoon, as Master Shen sat under the failing blossom tree, his humble robe mirroring the shades of sunset, a young monk named Li approached him, his face etched with concern. "Master Shen, why does the sight of this dying tree not bother you? You, who have always infused life into every withering soul, seem unperturbed by its suffering."

Master Shen replied, "Young Li, it is because I am embracing its dance with shadows - the dance of life." Confused, Li probed further, "But Master, the tree is dying. It's not dancing, it's dwindling. How can you be at peace with it?" Master Shen smiled gently, watching as the last of the cherry blossoms fell to the ground, their pink hue contrasting against the darkening earth. "Li, what you call dwindling, I see as a part of the tree's life cycle. It's merely changing its form, not disappearing."

"But Master, the tree won't bloom again, it won't spread its fragrance or give shade. Isn't it equivalent to disappearing?" Li asked, his voice trembling with despair. Master Shen picked up one of the fallen blossoms, now a faded pink, its delicate petals beginning to curl at the edges. With a soft sigh, he began to explain, "Li, every life, like this blossom, goes through stages of birth, growth, decay, and death. It's the dance of shadows and light, of appearing and disappearing. It's the rhythm of the universe itself, Li,"

Li was silent for a moment, then asked, "But, doesn't it make you sad, Master? Doesn't it make you want to prevent it?" Master Shen looked at the young monk, his smile gentle. "I won't deny the sadness, Li. It's natural to feel sorrow at the loss of something beautiful. However, trying to prevent it would be like trying to stop the sun from setting or the winter from coming. It would be denying the very nature of life. We must learn to accept and embrace impermanence."

"What do we gain from accepting impermanence, Master?" Li asked, his eyebrows furrowed in thought. "Freedom, Li," answered Master Shen. "The freedom from fear, from attachments, and from suffering. Once we accept that everything is transient, we learn to appreciate each moment, each breath, and each blossom before they wither."

Li looked at the withering tree and then at the fallen blossom in Master Shen's hand. His heart was heavy, yet he felt a strange sense of liberation. Master Shen got up slowly, the last rays of the setting sun casting long shadows. He turned to Li, his eyes reflecting the wisdom of the ages. "The tree may die, Li, but its seeds will sprout new life. Its essence will remain in the blossoms it has given and in the shade it has provided. Its dance with shadows will go on."

As Master Shen walked away, Li remained, his gaze fixed on the aged cherry blossom tree. The silence of the garden was only broken by the rustling of the leaves, whispering the wisdom of impermanence. He understood then, that accepting impermanence was not surrendering to despair, but finding peace and freedom in the ever-changing dance of life.

54

Bridge over Turbulent Waters: Connection Amidst Chaos

In the heart of a bustling city that never slept, adjacent to the dark alleyways and towering skyscrapers, there sat a serene, tranquil park. At the center of this oasis of calm, there was a vast stretch of a turbulent lake, its waters reflecting the chaotic metropolis. A wooden bridge, robust and timeless, served as the only passage across the unruly waters, connecting two parts of the park. On a typical afternoon, as the sun slid behind the gigantic buildings, casting long shadows and splattering the sky with orange streaks, a Zen Monk named Haku stepped onto the bridge. His steps were light, unhurried, his eyes, an infinite pool of calm. The wind played with the folds of his robe; the chaotic sounds of the city, a distant murmur.

On the other end of the bridge, a young businessman named Max hurriedly walked. His eyes darted in every direction and his mind raced with numerous worries, mirroring the chaotic city that surrounded him. His eyes flickered towards Haku as their paths were destined to cross on the bridge. The waters underneath roared in turmoil, mirroring the chaos in Max's soul. He hurled himself into busy schedules, daunting deadlines, and countless board meetings, just to drown the real chaos inside him, the real chaos that was himself.

Max glanced at the monk, noticing a stark contrast between their demeanors. Haku, despite moving in the same world, seemed untouched by the frenzied energy. His eyes met Max's and a knowing smile grazed his lips, as if he understood the turmoil mirrored in Max's frantic gaze. As they crossed paths, Max felt an indescribable pull towards the monk. An invisible bridge, stronger and more profound than the wooden one they crossed, seemed to connect them - two souls on opposite ends of the chaos spectrum. The connection felt warm, familiar, and ironically, peaceful amidst the chaos. It was the beginning of a journey for Max, a journey to find his own bridge over turbulent waters. Max followed Haku to the other side of the bridge, curiosity piqued. He observed the monk's calm demeanor in the middle of chaos, his assured strides, the serenity that seemed to envelop him like an invisible cloak. Intrigued, he decided to engage Haku in conversation.

"Excuse me, Monk," Max blurted out, "How can you maintain such calm in the midst of this chaos?" Haku paused and turned to Max, his calm gaze meeting the businessman's restless one. "By being like this bridge," he said, pointing towards the wooden structure behind them. "But the bridge is just a structure," Max protested, struggling to comprehend.

Haku nodded. "Indeed, the bridge is just a structure, but it serves as a connection between two worlds. Despite the turbulent waters beneath, it retains its peace. It allows the chaos to flow underneath without allowing it to affect its purpose. Such should be our approach to life's chaos. We shouldn't let it consume us. Instead, we should let it flow beneath us while we focus on our true purpose." Max stared at Haku, his eyes wide. He had spent years trying to control the chaos, only to realize that he should have let it pass, focusing on his own path instead. Haku's words struck him like a thunderbolt, demanding him to reassess his life and priorities.

From that day on, Max began to look at his life differently. He became more mindful of his reactions to the chaos around him, learning to embrace it rather than fight it. The stress and negativity that once consumed him began to subside steadily. His journey of self-discovery, guided by the wisdom of the Zen monk, allowed him to find joy and embrace his ideal life. The bridge over turbulent waters was no longer just a structure in a park, but a symbol of his newfound wisdom and the connection amidst chaos.

55

Flame and Wind's Tango: Harmonizing with Life's Currents.

$\mathcal{I}$n the heart of rural Japan, within a simple bamboo house, an old Zen monk, Genjo, lived in solitary serenity. His life was a testament to the beauty of simplicity, his wisdom a beacon to many in the village who often sought his advice, and his presence a sanctuary of tranquility. On one particular evening, he was seated by the hearth, brewing a pot of green tea. The flame beneath the pot danced and flickered, casting an aura of warmth and comfort around the room. Outside, the wind was whistling through the bamboo stalks, shaking their leaves in an age-old rhythm. Genjo admired the flame's dance, its gentle sway, and the radiating warmth it offered. He then turned his attention to the wind, its invisible presence felt through the rattling of bamboo stalks and the rustling leaves, full of resounding vigor. Both were contrasting, yet, they existed harmoniously, each in their own rhythm, their own dance of life.

A sudden gust of wind, stronger than before, made the flame quiver, threatening to blow it out. Genjo, noticing this, adjusted the hearth's window, sheltering the flame, yet allowing enough wind to keep the fire alive. After a moment, the flame regained its previous dance, now accompanied by a gentle breeze that slipped in through the narrow opening. Just then, there was a knock on the door. With the famous smile etched on his face, Genjo rose to greet his visitor. It was Hayato, a young man from the village. His eyes were low, reflecting a troubled mind, and his usual cheerful visage was replaced by a look of desolation. Noting this, Genjo gestured for him to sit by the hearth, and with a calm voice, offered him a cup of freshly brewed tea. As Hayato took the cup, he looked at Genjo with pleading eyes, silently asking for guidance. Genjo, understanding the unspoken request, turned his gaze back to the flame and the wind, preparing to share another nugget of wisdom from his life's reservoir.

Genjo paused, sipped his tea, then spoke. "Hayato, observe the flame and the wind. They seem at odds, don't they? The flame wants to rise and dance, while the wind blows with a force that could extinguish it. But look closer. The wind fuels the flame, giving it the oxygen necessary to burn. The flame, in turn, yields to the wind's direction, going where it is guided."

Hayato watched as Genjo gestured toward the flickering flame. His voice held a gentle rhythm, like the rustling bamboo outside. "The flame and the wind are not enemies but partners in a beautiful dance. They learn from each other. They adapt, harmonize, and survive. The flame could disappear when faced with a powerful gust, yet it persists, understanding the wind's nature, and the wind, in turn, fuels the flame, recognizing its potential." Genjo turned to face Hayato, his eyes shining with the wisdom of a thousand suns. "In life, we too are faced with winds that threaten to put out our flame, winds of hardship, suffering, and discomfort. We may not have control over them, but we can choose how we dance with them. We can choose to resist, to fight against the direction of the wind, or we can choose to yield, to learn from it, to let it guide us."

Hayato listened closely, taking in each word. His eyes shifted from the flame to Genjo, a spark of understanding starting to twinkle. "The secret is not in dousing the winds of life but rather learning to dance with them. Allow them to strengthen your flame, to fuel your growth, just as the flame does. In this way, Hayato, you will find that even the toughest winds serve a purpose and bring with them lessons of resilience, strength, and wisdom." With these words, Genjo finished his tea, offering Hayato a final smile. His gaze turned back to the flame and the wind outside, two forces of nature dancing together in perfect harmony.

Disclaimer

The Zen Monk and the Blossoming Lotus Flower: 55 Stories for Stress Relief, Conquering Negativity, Discovering Joy, and Embracing Your Ideal Life is a work of fiction and self-help literature created for entertainment, inspiration, and personal growth. While the stories, advice, and techniques presented in this book draw from principles of mindfulness, meditation, and positive psychology, they are not a substitute for professional advice or treatment.

Readers are encouraged to consult with qualified healthcare professionals, therapists, or counselors for specific guidance on their individual challenges, mental health, or well-being. The author and publisher of this book are not responsible for any actions taken by readers based on the content of this book.

The anecdotes and characters in this book are fictional, and any resemblance to real persons, living or dead, is purely coincidental. The author has drawn from various sources of inspiration, including traditional wisdom, personal experiences, and imagination, to craft the stories and concepts presented within.

The Zen Monk and the Blossoming Lotus Flower is intended to provide readers with tools and perspectives to help manage stress, negativity, and cultivate a more joyful and purposeful life. However, the effectiveness of these tools may vary from person to person, and results are not guaranteed.

By reading this book, you acknowledge that you are responsible for your own choices and actions, and you agree to use the information within for personal growth and self-improvement purposes. The author and publisher disclaim any liability arising directly or indirectly from the use of this book.

Please read and apply the content of this book mindfully and responsibly, and seek professional guidance when necessary. Enjoy your journey toward a more balanced and fulfilling life.

Made in United States
Orlando, FL
07 November 2023

38603630R00086